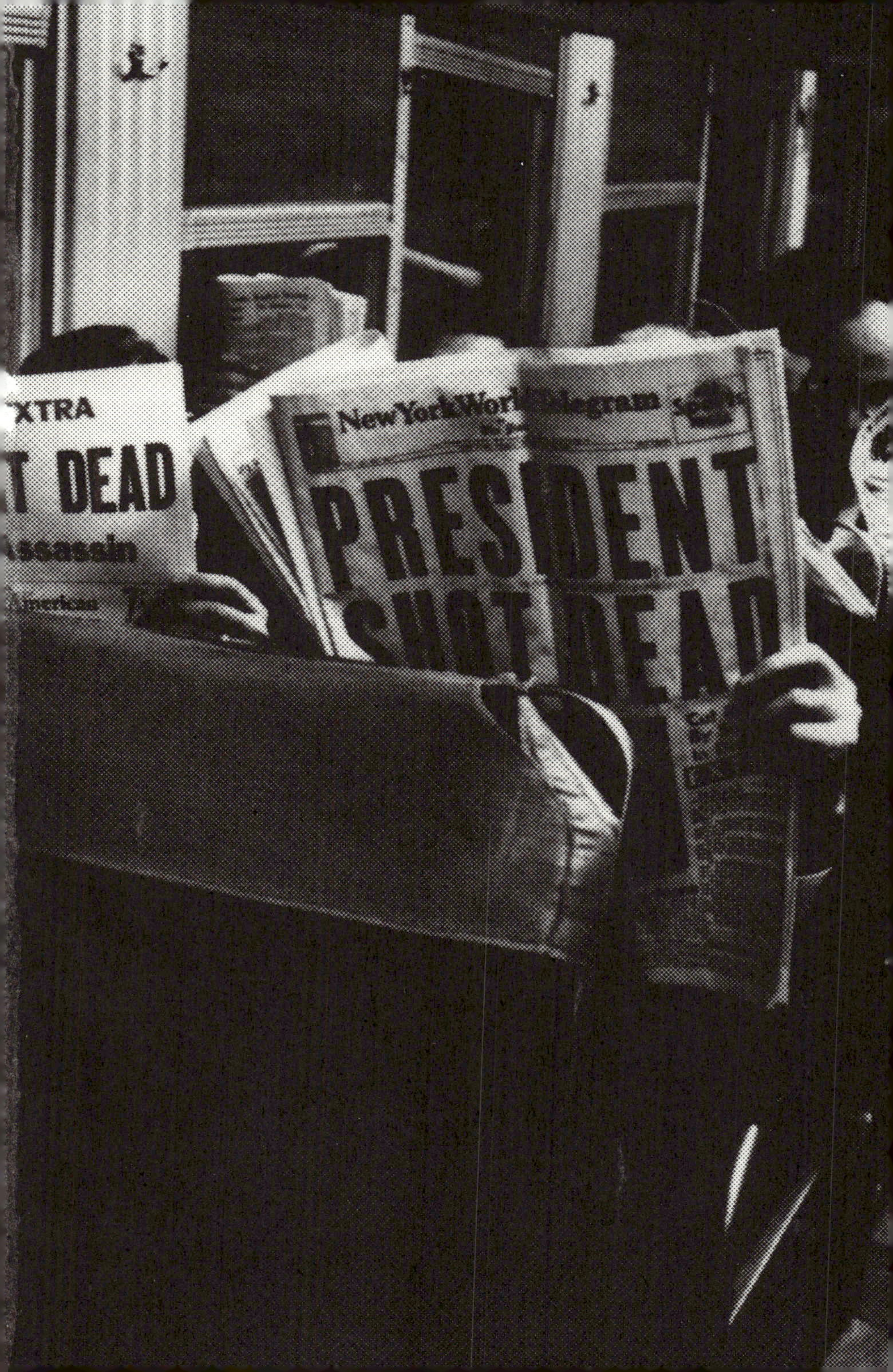
XTRA
T DEAD
PRESIDENT

"THE **PRESI**

SCHOLASTIC PRESS | NEW YORK

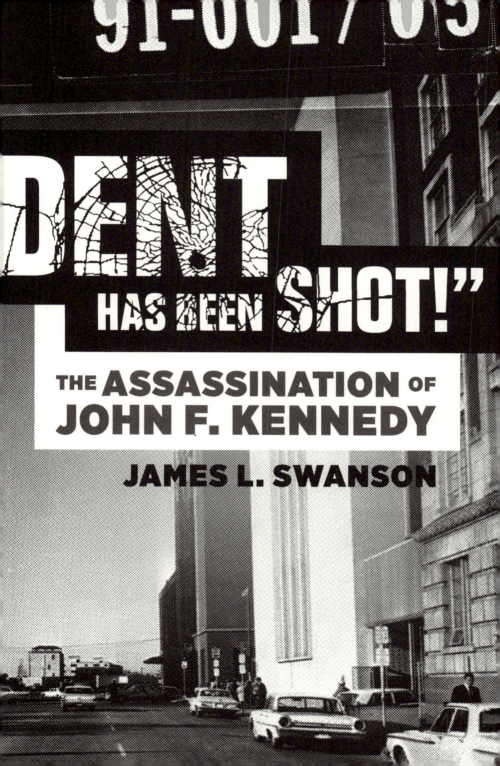

91-001/05

"...DENT HAS BEEN SHOT!"

THE ASSASSINATION OF JOHN F. KENNEDY

JAMES L. SWANSON

Library of Congress Cataloging-in-Publication Data

Swanson, James L., 1959–
"The president has been shot!" : the assassination
of John F. Kennedy/by James L. Swanson. —
First edition. pages cm.
Includes bibliographical references and index.
ISBN 978-0-545-49007-8 (hardcover :alk. paper)
1. Kennedy, John F. (John Fitzgerald), 1917–1963 —
Assassination — Juvenile literature. I. Title.
E842.9.S95 2013

973.922092 — dc23

2012041167

10 9 8 7 6 5 4 3 2 1   13 14 15 16 17

Printed in the U.S.A.   23
First edition, October 2013

The display type was set in Gotham.
The text was set in Adobe Garamond.
Book design by Phil Falco

FOR ANDREA AND
MY FATHER, LENNART

TABLE OF CONTENTS

John and Jacqueline Kennedy playing with baby Caroline in front of their Georgetown house in 1960.

BEGINNINGS

Historic Georgetown, in the northwest section of Washington, DC, is one of the most prestigious neighborhoods in the nation's capital. Founded as a commercial trading hub along the banks of the Potomac River before the American Revolution, Georgetown boasts the oldest home in Washington, along with many other eighteenth-century brick town houses.

Over the past two centuries, many distinguished Americans—congressmen, senators, judges, federal officials, military officers, authors, and one man who would become president—have called Georgetown home. In its long history, no public figure has been more connected to the neighborhood than John F. Kennedy, the thirty-fifth president of the United States.

He lived in several homes in Georgetown beginning in 1946, during the time when he gained national recognition as a U.S. congressman and senator, married Jacqueline Bouvier, and, in November 1960, was elected president. Between his election and his inauguration on January 20, 1961, the circa 1811 three-story Federal-era brick town house at 3307 N Street NW served as a nerve center. There John Kennedy planned and hired staff for his forthcoming administration, which he called "the New Frontier."

For two and a half months, the lights burned late as the president-elect gathered his closest advisers around him.

The Kennedys leave their Georgetown home for preinaugural festivities on the snowy night of January 19, 1961.

Journalists camped outside the home to photograph or film Kennedy. They were there whenever he opened the front door, stood on the top step, and walked down to the public sidewalk a few feet in front of the house to announce the new appointment of a person to his administration.

On January 19, the night before his inauguration, a heavy snowstorm paralyzed the nation's capital. The glow from the pair of clear glass and black metal lamps flanking John Kennedy's front door made the crystals layering the surface of the deep snow twinkle in the night. Undeterred by the weather, the Kennedys ventured out to attend long-planned pre-inauguration parties. Jacqueline Kennedy wore a shimmering white floor-length ball gown that mirrored the soft, thick snowy carpet that covered the capital. A photograph captured her as she walked through her front door and stepped into the night. Surrounded by darkness, she shone as bright as a glimmering star.

The next morning, John and Jacqueline Kennedy left their house for the last time and embarked on a journey that he would not complete, and from which he would never return.

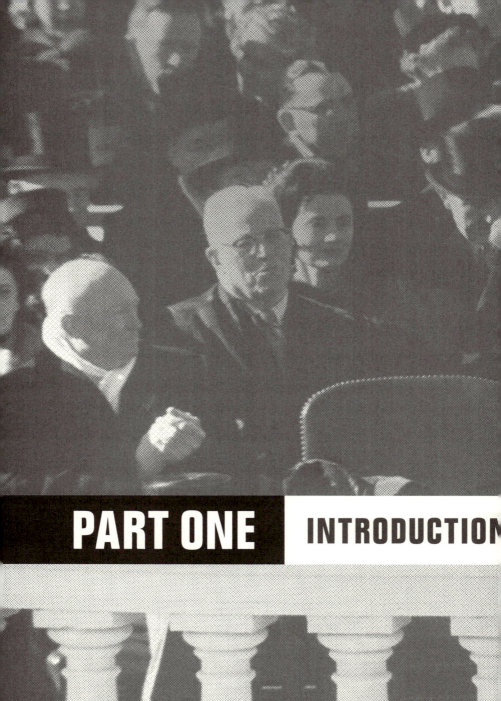

PART ONE INTRODUCTION

TO JOHN F. KENNEDY

THE EARLY YEARS

John F. Kennedy remains the youngest man ever elected president of the United States. Born in Brookline, Massachusetts, in May 1917, the year America entered the First World War, young John had political blood in his veins. His maternal grandfather, John "Honey Fitz" Fitzgerald, had been a Democratic mayor of Boston. And his own father, Joseph P. Kennedy, served in President Franklin Roosevelt's administration as ambassador to Great Britain in the years leading up to the Second World War. These achievements were great honors for an Irish Catholic family that had been treated as second-class citizens by the snobbish New England elite.

Joseph Kennedy was a self-made millionaire, and he raised his nine children — including four sons — in an atmosphere of wealth and privilege. Joseph Kennedy vowed that one day his eldest son, Joe Jr., would become the first Catholic president of the United States, and he prepared him for success. In World War II, Joe Jr. was a bomber pilot and served in Europe, fighting Nazi Germany.

John, Joseph's second-eldest son, known as Jack to friends and family, became a navy lieutenant and served in the Pacific theater, fighting the Japanese. Jack commanded a PT boat, a small, fast craft with a wood hull that was designed to approach

The Kennedy family in 1931, including eight of the nine children. From left to right: Robert Kennedy, John F. Kennedy, Eunice Kennedy, Jean Kennedy (on lap of) Joseph P. Kennedy Sr., Rose Fitzgerald Kennedy (behind) Patricia Kennedy, Kathleen Kennedy, Joseph P. Kennedy Jr. (behind) Rosemary Kennedy. Edward Kennedy was not yet born.

John Kennedy (far right) during World War II aboard his boat, *PT-109*, with his crew.

much larger Japanese warships and attack them with torpedoes. Jack narrowly escaped death on August 2, 1943, when, at 2:30 in the morning, an enemy ship rammed and sliced his boat, *PT-109*, in half. Two of his twelve crewmen were killed, and he and several others were injured. In darkness, they clung to the wreckage that remained afloat. After it was light, Kennedy led his crew on a swim to a tiny, deserted island. One man, suffering from bad burns, could not make it. Jack refused to abandon him to die, so he clenched in his teeth a strap connected to the sailor's life jacket, and for four grueling hours, he towed the man behind him until they reached land. That night, although exhausted, Kennedy volunteered to swim out alone with the hope of sighting an American vessel that could rescue them. He planned to fire his revolver and signal with a flashlight. But no ship passed his way. After spending hours in the water, he returned the next day and collapsed on the beach.

Soon Kennedy led his men on a swim to another island, where they found hospitable natives. Kennedy carved a message on a coconut shell that the islanders carried to friendly military forces. He and his men were rescued. War had tested the limits of John Kennedy's physical and mental endurance, and he passed that test with great courage and coolness in the face of danger. Later, when he was president, Kennedy displayed that coconut on his desk as a treasured souvenir of his escape from death.

His brother Joe Jr. was not so lucky. In 1944, Joe's plane exploded over the English Channel during a dangerous mission, and he was killed. Ambassador Kennedy told a reluctant Jack that it was up to him now—he must take his older brother's place, achieve great things, and fulfill his father's dream of starting a political dynasty.

In 1946, one year after the end of World War II, John Kennedy ran for the United States House of Representatives as a Democrat. He was an awkward campaigner and not a natural politician. That would come later, with experience. But voters admired his military service, and they put him over the top. After winning reelection in 1948 and 1950, he ran for and won a seat in the United States Senate in 1952.

In September 1953, at the age of thirty-six, he married Jacqueline Lee Bouvier, an attractive, educated, and well-bred twenty-four-year-old former debutante who had, like him, been raised to assume a place among the wealthy American elite. Their wedding in Newport, Rhode Island, was the social event of the season. But soon Jack faced death again. Plagued by

Newly married, Senator John F. Kennedy and his bride, Jacqueline Bouvier, cut their wedding cake.

painful back injuries he had had since his youth, and made worse during the war, he underwent a series of agonizing surgeries to cure the problem. He almost died, but he struggled to live, and survived. For the rest of his life, he suffered from terrible pain—and other serious illnesses, including Addison's disease—that he concealed with a cheerful public demeanor.

THE 1960 ELECTION

In January 1960, Kennedy declared himself a candidate for the Democratic nomination for president of the United States. He outmaneuvered his older and more experienced rivals, including Senator Lyndon Baines Johnson of Texas, the powerful Senate majority leader, and won the nomination.

The Republicans nominated former Senator Richard Nixon of California, who had, for the past seven years, served as vice president of the United States under the popular President Dwight Eisenhower, the victorious Supreme Allied Commander during the Second World War. Kennedy and Nixon shared many similarities. Both had served as navy officers in the war, both had been elected to Congress in 1946, and then to the Senate. There they worked cordially with each other, shared an interest in foreign affairs, and agreed on one of the great issues of the day—the danger posed by Communism and the Soviet Union.

But in another way, they could not have been more different. John Kennedy's family was rich, and he had enjoyed all the privileges that money could buy—a fine Harvard education, world travel, material possessions, leisure, and his father's contacts. John Kennedy never had and never would need to work for a living a day in his life. His father wanted to free his sons from that pressure so that they could pursue political careers.

Richard Nixon, by contrast, came from a poor family and grew up without privilege. Whatever he had in life—a college education, a law degree, and a political office—he had to earn on his own with hard work and a keen mind. What John Kennedy was given, Richard Nixon had struggled to attain.

In college, Kennedy was an indifferent student, but he developed a love of American and European history. As a junior congressman, he earned a reputation as a young playboy, unserious about his work. But by the time he captured the Democratic nomination, he had evolved into a mature leader who, like Nixon, was a voracious reader, a savvy politician, and a formidable debater. Both men possessed brilliant minds.

The presidential election of 1960 turned out to be one of the closest in American history. Nixon entered the contest as the favorite. He possessed a track record of significant achievements, and the majority of voters respected his years of experience as President Eisenhower's vice president. One of the top issues of the day was preventing the spread of Communism around the world and curbing the influence of America's rival superpower, the Soviet Union. And Richard Nixon had unsurpassed credentials as an anti-Communist politician whose views were respected by the majority of Americans.

The main author of Communism was the nineteenth-century German philosopher Karl Marx, who believed that every individual must give way to the collective. Marx advocated the abolition of private property and organized religion, which he called the "opiate of the people." The most sustained effort to put Communism into practice began with the Russian Revolution of 1917 under the dictators Vladimir Lenin and, later,

Joseph Stalin. Communists claimed that their philosophy, when put into practice, would serve the common good. It proved to be a naive dream that was soon corrupted. Millions of people who resisted Communism in Russia and some thirty other countries throughout the twentieth century were killed—more than one hundred million victims in all. In pursuit of their goal, Communists established totalitarian political regimes that flouted individual rights, banned freedom of speech, eliminated free elections, set up police states, corrupted the rule of law, and imprisoned and murdered opponents.

World War II had ended with the defeat of Nazi Germany, Fascist Italy, and Imperial Japan by the Allies (who consisted of the United States, Great Britain, France, and the Soviet Union). With Germany and the Axis powers crushed, the Allies emerged as the great political powers of the postwar era. Of the Allied powers, only the Soviet Union was a Communist nation and not a democracy. The end of the war resulted in a delicate balance of power—a cold war in which no shots were fired—between the democratic nations and the Soviet Union. Former British Prime Minister Winston Churchill warned in a famous speech that an "iron curtain" now divided Europe into the free, democratic nations in the west, and the totalitarian, Communist nations in the east.

Richard Nixon owed his meteoric political career to his vigorous anti-Communism at the height of the Cold War. But some Americans thought that Nixon had gone too far, and they associated him with what they believed were excesses committed at home by Senator Joseph McCarthy and the House Un-American Activities Committee during their investigations of

Communists in the United States during the 1950s.

John Kennedy, too, began the race for the presidency with some disadvantages. No Catholic had ever been elected president. In that era, a prejudice that does not exist today might have prevented a person of that faith from becoming president. Kennedy argued that he would not be a "Catholic president" but merely a president who happened to be Catholic. He persuaded enough people that a person's religious beliefs should not bar him from the office.

Kennedy's other disadvantage was his lack of experience. Yes, he had served in the House and the Senate for fourteen years when he began his race for the presidency, but he was not particularly accomplished as a legislator. Nixon's supporters portrayed Kennedy as a callow young man who was only forty-three years old and who had not taken his time in Congress seriously. They argued that due to his lack of experience, he was unqualified to serve as president. Indeed, fellow Democrat Lyndon Johnson referred to Kennedy as a "boy." Johnson believed that Kennedy should wait his turn, until he was more mature, and not challenge him now for the nomination. Kennedy disagreed. He believed in the power of fate, and that his illnesses, injuries, and near-death experiences had marked him as a man who might be deprived of a long life. He was a man of action, determined to make the most of his time, and who wanted to accomplish things now.

In a series of televised debates between the two parties' presidential candidates — the first in American history — Kennedy leveled the playing field as seventy million people watched. Nixon was famous as a relentless and ruthless debater, and many

Vice President Richard M. Nixon and Senator John F. Kennedy dur

expected him to vanquish Kennedy. But before the evening of the first debate, Kennedy relaxed, shaved closely, and allowed stage makeup to be applied to his face. Nixon spent the day campaigning, and had aggravated a painful leg injury. He showed up at the television studio with a day's growth of beard, a five o'clock shadow. He refused makeup. People who listened to the debate on the radio thought that Nixon had won. Those who watched it on television, however, thought that Kennedy had won.

John Kennedy had a brilliant insight. He recognized that television would change political campaigns forever. Once, all that mattered was what a candidate said. Now it mattered just as much how he looked while he was saying it. During the first debate, John Kennedy looked relaxed, fit, and charismatic. Richard Nixon looked uncomfortable, swarthy, and nervous as he sweated under the hot lights. Kennedy also looked much younger, even though Nixon was only four years older than he. In content, the debate was almost a draw. The performances of the candidates were evenly matched. In the end, it was not necessary for John Kennedy to "win" the debate on the issues. It was enough that he looked like he belonged on the same stage with Richard Nixon. He did.

When Americans went to the polls on November 8, 1960, no great issues divided the candidates. Both men advocated strong missile defense against the Soviet threat. Kennedy was as anti-Communist as Nixon: both opposed its expansion, including in Cuba, an island ninety miles off the coast of Florida, and both saw the Soviet Union as a dangerous rival. Neither candidate was then at the forefront of the civil rights movement.

Voters chose between the personalities of the two men, as much as they did between the issues. Kennedy presented himself as the voice of a new generation who would get the country "moving" again toward a "new frontier." Nixon argued that he, not Kennedy, had the proven leadership experience to guide the nation in a dangerous world. Out of 68.3 million votes cast, John Kennedy received only about 119,450 more votes than Richard Nixon. Nixon had lost the presidency by just two-tenths of 1 percent of the popular vote. It was one of the closest elections in history.

Late into the night, neither man knew who had won. Not until the morning after the election was Kennedy declared the winner.

THE INAUGURATION

On January 20, 1961, John Fitzgerald Kennedy stepped forward on the East Front of the U.S. Capitol to take the oath of office as the thirty-fifth president of the United States and to deliver his inaugural address. Half of America had voted against him, but on this day, he behaved and spoke with confidence. Although he knew that he had not won by a large margin at the polls, he sought to win a mandate now with his words. He summoned the American people to stand up for freedom in the shadow of the Cold War.

> *Let the word go forth from this time and place, to friend and foe alike, that the torch has been passed to a new generation of Americans—born in this century, tempered by war, disciplined by a hard and bitter peace, proud of our ancient heritage and unwilling to witness or permit the slow undoing of those human rights to which this nation has always been committed, and to which we are committed today at home and around the world.*

He cautioned other countries not to doubt his commitment to freedom in what he predicted would be a "long twilight struggle."

> *Let every nation know, whether it wishes us well or ill, that we shall pay any price, bear any burden, meet any hardship, support any friend, oppose any foe, to assure the survival and the success of liberty.*

Then he suggested that nations pursue peaceful cooperation, not military confrontation.

Together let us explore the stars, conquer the deserts, eradicate disease, tap the ocean depths, and encourage the arts and commerce.

He reminded his audience that this would take time.

All this will not be finished in the first one hundred days. Nor will it be finished in the first one thousand days, nor in the life of this administration, nor even, perhaps, in our lifetime on this planet. But let us begin.

Kennedy suggested that his election coincided with a special moment in history.

In the long history of the world, only a few generations have been granted the role of defending freedom in its hour of maximum danger. I do not shrink from this responsibility—I welcome it. I do not believe that any of us would exchange places with any other people or any other generation. The energy, the faith, the devotion which we bring to this endeavor will light our country and all who serve it—and the glow from that fire can truly light the world.

Perhaps the most quoted and famous line from the speech is Kennedy's call to self-sacrifice.

And so, my fellow Americans, ask not what your country can do for you—ask what you can do for your country.

President Kennedy delivers his inaugural address, January 20, 1961.

THE BAY OF PIGS

Foreign affairs and fighting the spread of Communism around the world dominated John Kennedy's first two years in office. He was a Cold Warrior who had a personal fascination with counterinsurgency warfare, covert action, and special military forces, including the Green Berets, a small, elite unit of the U.S. Army. A fan of Ian Fleming's James Bond novels, President Kennedy had an instinctive and enthusiastic appetite for secret operations. He also had an obsession with Cuba and with its leader, Fidel Castro.

A revolutionary who overthrew the Cuban government in 1959, Castro seemed at first that he might turn to America for inspiration and support. Instead he turned to the Communist Soviet Union for aid and set himself up as the repressive dictator of his nation.

During the administration of President Eisenhower, the Central Intelligence Agency (CIA) had developed a secret plan to help anti-Castro Cuban exiles—living outside Cuba, trained and equipped by the United States—to invade their homeland, depose Castro, and overturn Communism. The CIA asked Kennedy to approve it.

Kennedy authorized what became known as the Bay of Pigs operation, named for the place in Cuba where the armed exiles would land. The invasion, on April 17, 1961, was a catastrophe.

Cuban leader Fidel Castro embraces premier of the Soviet Union Nikita Khrushchev.

The fourteen hundred freedom fighters, heavily outnumbered, found Castro's troops waiting for them. Within two days, most had been captured, wounded, or killed. The CIA and the U.S. military had persuaded President Kennedy to support the plan by arguing that its success would not require him to send American troops or air support into battle against Castro's forces. They predicted that the invasion would trigger a spontaneous uprising by the Cuban people against their leader.

That revolt never happened. The assurances by CIA officials and military generals had proven wildly optimistic — even deluded — and now they implored Kennedy to commit American forces to save the catastrophic operation. He refused. He feared that it might trigger a direct military conflict with the Soviet Union. The CIA plan had failed. It had been a humiliating disaster that would haunt his presidency. But Kennedy accepted responsibility for it and learned a valuable lesson: in the future, he would be more skeptical of overconfident promises made by his military and intelligence advisers.

The Bay of Pigs episode did not stop the CIA from developing other secret plans — including one called Operation Mongoose — to overthrow or even assassinate Fidel Castro. Kennedy worried that Cuba might influence or contaminate Latin America with Communism.

Nor did the Cuban failure deter Kennedy from opposing the spread of Communism in Southeast Asia. When Kennedy took office, there were several hundred American military advisers in Vietnam. He increased their number to seventeen thousand, believing that America should make a stand against Communism there to prevent the ideology from conquering not just Vietnam but also neighboring countries.

In 1961, to prepare for the challenges ahead, President Kennedy asked Congress to increase the size and budget of the U.S. military. To promote peace and international cooperation, he also inspired thousands of young Americans to join public service by establishing the Peace Corps, an organization to help developing countries improve their public health, education, and agriculture. He wanted America to look both merciful and mighty.

THE CUBAN
MISSILE CRISIS

Eighteen months after the Bay of Pigs, the United States and the
Soviet Union almost went to war over another confrontation in
Cuba. In October 1962, American spy planes detected the presence of Russian missile bases under construction there. The short
distance between the island nation and the United States meant
that, from these sites, Cuba or Russia could launch nuclear missiles at major cities and military bases in the eastern United
States. The Soviets had sent missiles to Cuba to deter any future
invasion of the island by the United States, and because, beginning in 1961, the U.S. had deployed in Italy and Turkey nuclear
missiles that could be launched to attack the Soviet Union.

Kennedy revealed the frightening discovery in Cuba in a
televised address. He warned that he would not tolerate nuclear
missiles in Cuba. The volatile Russian leader, Nikita Khrushchev,
had assumed, after the Bay of Pigs affair and an unimpressive
personal meeting with Kennedy two months later, that the
young president was weak and would do nothing when the Soviets parked their missiles in Cuba. Over thirteen days — from
October 16 to 28, 1962 — the United States and the Soviet
Union came close to nuclear war during what became known as
the Cuban Missile Crisis.

Many of Kennedy's advisers urged him to attack Cuba at

Aerial surveillance photos document the presence of missile sites in Cuba.

A newspaper cartoon published during the Cuban Missile Crisis illustrates the danger of the confrontation. John Kennedy and Nikita Khrushchev sit atop hydrogen bombs, their fingers inches from the buttons that will start a nuclear war.

once, first bombing the missile bases and then invading the island. Knowing that such a rash response might provoke war with Russia, Kennedy took his time, delaying his decision, and hoping for a diplomatic solution. In the meantime, he ordered a naval quarantine around Cuba and declared that no Soviet ships carrying missiles or military supplies would be allowed to approach the island. At the last minute, to avoid a war, Khrushchev ordered his ships to turn back. But that alone did not end the crisis. Kennedy and Khrushchev negotiated a settlement: the United States agreed to remove its missiles from Turkey and promised not to invade Cuba. In return, the Russians agreed to remove their missiles from Cuba. President Kennedy had taken the United States and the Soviet Union to the brink of a nuclear war in which millions might have perished, but he had solved the dispute in a responsible manner. The most dangerous crisis of his presidency was over.

THE SPACE RACE

The competition between democracy and Communism—between the United States and the Soviet Union—was not limited to Cuba, Southeast Asia, Eastern Europe, or even to planet Earth. Each superpower believed it could tip the balance of influence in its own favor by placing satellites in space and men on the moon. National pride was at stake: which country would be the first to launch a rocket into space and spin a satellite in orbit around Earth? This "space race" captured Kennedy's imagination. The Soviet Union had already beaten America into space when it launched the first satellite, *Sputnik 1*, in 1957. Then, on April 12, 1961, the Russians launched the first man into space. These successes shocked the American people. For reasons of prestige, and also national security, President Kennedy decided that America must catch up.

On May 25, 1961, the president addressed both the House and the Senate—a joint session of Congress: "I believe that this nation should commit itself to achieving the goal, before this decade is out, of landing a man on the moon and returning him safely to the earth. No single space project in this period will be more impressive to mankind or more important for the long-range exploration of space."

Later, in a speech on September 12, 1962, Kennedy emphasized the importance of the issue: "No nation which expects to

In 1961, Alan Shepard was the first American to travel in space.

be the leader of other nations can expect to stay behind in this race for space. . . . We choose to go to the moon in this decade and do the other things, not because they are easy, but because they are hard." Inspired and supported by President Kennedy, the National Aeronautics and Space Administration (NASA), the agency in charge of America's space program, recruited more astronauts, designed giant rockets, and planned the Mercury, Gemini, and Apollo space programs.

BERLIN

In 1963, Kennedy's focus on foreign affairs gave him two of the greatest pleasures of his presidency, the first occurring in Berlin. In 1945, at the end of World War II, a treaty signed by the Allies divided all of Germany into zones of occupation. The zones controlled by the United States, Great Britain, and France became known as West Germany, and the zone controlled by the Soviet Union became known as East Germany. Berlin, the national capital, was within the Russian zone, and the city was divided into four sectors, each occupied by a different Allied power.

In 1963, the Soviet Union still controlled eastern Germany. Indeed, in August 1961, during the first year of Kennedy's presidency, the Soviets built a concrete and barbed-wire wall between their area and West Berlin to prevent the population of the Soviet sector from fleeing Communism and escaping to the western zones. During the existence of that wall, Russian and Soviet-controlled East German soldiers shot to death several hundred men, women, and teenagers who tried to cross over it to freedom.

On June 26, 1963, President Kennedy stood on the free side of the Berlin Wall and spoke to a throng of 300,000 people in the square. "Freedom has many difficulties," he said, "and democracy is not perfect, but we have never had to put a wall

President Kennedy speaks in Berlin, June 26, 1963.

up to keep our people in." He told the massive, cheering crowd that "all free men, wherever they live, are citizens of Berlin, and therefore, as a free man, I take pride in the words *'Ich bin ein Berliner.'*" That meant that he too was a citizen of Berlin. He had touched the German people with his empathy. And he told people around the world that if they wanted to understand the difference between Communism and freedom, "let them come to Berlin." The ecstatic crowd was the largest one that Kennedy had ever addressed. It was the high point of his worldwide popularity, and he said that he could not imagine enjoying a better day than this.

In November 1951, the United States tested a nuclear bomb by detonating it in a remote part of Nevada. The United States and the Soviet Union went on to explode many nuclear weapons in the atmosphere. President Kennedy sought to ban the practice.

THE NUCLEAR TEST BAN TREATY

Kennedy also worried about the proliferation of nuclear weapons among the superpowers. The United States and the Soviet Union possessed arsenals of several thousand nuclear weapons. Most of them were more powerful and destructive than the two atomic bombs that the United States dropped on Hiroshima and Nagasaki, Japan, in 1945, to end the Second World War. Through the 1940s, 1950s, and 1960s, the nations that possessed nuclear weapons tested their effectiveness and demonstrated their military superiority by exploding them in their own territory, either underground, in the ocean, or in the atmosphere in remote areas far removed from population centers. Nonetheless, the tests still resulted in radioactive fallout, which winds and weather systems could carry for hundreds of miles and contaminate the food supply, or towns and cities. Kennedy negotiated with the Soviet Union to end atmospheric testing, and in October 1963, he signed a Limited Nuclear Test Ban Treaty. He considered it the most significant achievement of his presidency.

CIVIL RIGHTS

Domestic issues captivated John Kennedy less than foreign affairs, although he was keen to reduce individual federal income tax rates and also corporate taxes, which he believed were too high and stifled the economy. There was one domestic issue that, above all others, he wanted to avoid: the fight for civil rights for African Americans.

Kennedy was not, of course, against civil rights. He was not one of the Southerners who had disagreed with the Supreme Court's ruling in *Brown v. Board of Education*, the school desegregation case in which the Court declared it unconstitutional to ban black children from attending public schools with white children. Nor did he want, as did many Southern members of his own party, to suppress other rights of citizenship, including voting, attending public universities, or patronizing restaurants, shops, and hotels. During the century since the Civil War and the end of slavery, African Americans had not enjoyed equal rights. Segregation and suppression were rampant. But Kennedy worried that becoming a civil rights champion was premature, and that doing so would stir up political opposition among Southern Democrats and endanger the programs and legislation that he wanted Congress to approve. Vice President Lyndon Johnson was, by contrast, a more enthusiastic advocate for civil rights; however, his authority was limited.

But a series of events made it impossible for John Kennedy to keep the civil rights movement at arm's length anymore. In September 1962, he was forced to send federal troops to the University of Mississippi to suppress rioting that ensued when a black man named James Meredith was threatened with death after he tried to enroll as a student there. In May 1963, Americans—including President Kennedy—watched on television as Eugene "Bull" Connor, Commissioner of Public Safety in Birmingham, Alabama, turned dogs and fire hoses on civil rights demonstrators. Then Governor George Wallace refused to desegregate the University of Alabama, blocking the entrance with his own body.

John Kennedy decided he could not wait any longer. Ugly images of racist white mobs were broadcast all over the world, exposing the evil of racial discrimination in "the land of the free." This played into Communist propaganda that the United States was the land of hypocrisy and oppression of blacks, not liberty. On June 11, 1963, Kennedy gave a televised address to the nation on civil rights.

"This is not a sectional issue," he said, not wanting to single out and inflame the South. He knew that blacks also received poor treatment in the North. Indeed, Martin Luther King Jr. would say that when he led civil rights demonstrations in Chicago, the racism he encountered there was as vicious as anything he had seen in the Deep South. "This is not even a legal or legislative issue alone," Kennedy continued. "We are confronted primarily with a moral issue. It is as old as the Scriptures and as clear as the American Constitution."

On August 28, 1963, civil rights demonstrators staged a march

Snarling police dogs attack a nonviolent civil rights demonstrator in Birmingham, Alabama. This photo, published across the country and around the world, harmed America's reputation.

President Kennedy and Vice President Johnson (second from right) meet in the White House with Martin Luther King Jr. (far left) and other civil rights leaders on the afternoon of the March on Washington, August 1963.

on Washington, DC, where two hundred and fifty thousand people heard Martin Luther King Jr. deliver his famous "I Have a Dream" speech atop the steps of the Lincoln Memorial. President Kennedy had also been asked to speak, but declined an invitation. From the White House, he watched on television as King spoke. Kennedy had hoped that the march would never happen, preferring that the civil rights movement use laws and legislation, and not huge public protests, to achieve its goals. And if the march became unruly or violent, Kennedy was prepared to intervene to stop it. But the event was peaceful, and it was the crowning moment of Dr. King's life. Later in the day, Kennedy received King and other civil rights leaders at the White House. Kennedy knew that times were changing and that history was on the side of the civil rights movement. He knew that from this moment on, he would have to make it a priority, and that ensuring equal rights for black Americans must become a goal during his second term, once he won reelection in 1964.

THE KENNEDY MYSTIQUE

By the summer of 1963, John Kennedy's presidency had hit its stride. Back in 1961, he'd had a shaky start in office. But he'd overcome the humiliating failure of the Bay of Pigs invasion and had grown in maturity and confidence. He had gone on to keep Russian missiles out of Cuba without provoking a nuclear war, he'd set the United States on an epic journey to the moon, he'd achieved a historic nuclear test ban treaty, and he'd gone to Berlin, symbol of the Cold War, where he'd denounced the evils of Communism in a speech that had inspired people around the world.

To many Americans, there was more to his administration—something intangible—than speeches, world travels, multiple crises, and anti-Communism. He had style. Kennedy possessed a glamorous effervescence that made him seem larger than life and a youthful symbol of a new era of American optimism and spirit. He was the first president born in the twentieth century. Now in his third year in office, he was still only forty-six. With his enchanting wife, who was just thirty-four, and two beautiful young children, the telegenic president cultivated a jaunty, athletic public image of a sailor, touch-football enthusiast, sportsman, and father. The public nicknamed him "JFK."

Jacqueline Kennedy—or Jackie, as she was known—became a star in her own right. Sometimes she even outshone JFK himself. Celebrated for her elegant, trendsetting fashion and understated

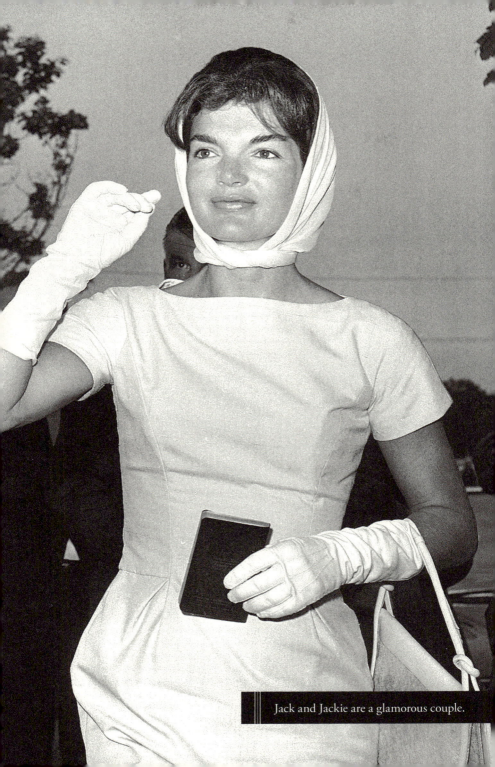
Jack and Jackie are a glamorous couple.

beauty, she appeared on the covers of magazines looking more like an alluring movie actress than a politician's wife. She was a world traveler and lover of culture. And yet she remained a reserved, quiet person whose desire for privacy made her all the more fascinating to the public. A strong believer in the preservation of America's past, she undertook a much-needed historic renovation of the White House, hosted a popular and unprecedented television special on the result, and brought the president's home alive with artists, authors, and musicians.

John Kennedy's sharp wit and ability to laugh at himself enhanced his appeal. But he had a dark side. He loved history for its lessons and inspiration, but he was also drawn to its fatalism, irony, and disappointments. And below the surface of his public image of vigor, his good cheer camouflaged a lifetime of physical pain and illness. Convinced that the American people did not want to see their president as weak or sick, he battled his ailments in secret. Of all his characteristics, John Kennedy had one more important than all the rest—an ability to inspire people, through words and personal example, to attempt great things. It was the core of his mystique.

It was the fall of 1963. The presidential election of November 1964 was just one year away. Kennedy planned to run for a second term, and hoped to win by a margin wider than he had eked out in 1960. It was essential that he again win the state of Texas. In 1963, warring factions of the liberal and conservative wings of the Democratic party in that state were at each other's throats, fighting over which group would control politics in the state. JFK wanted the dispute to end. To increase his chances for reelection, he decided to travel to Texas in late November to campaign with Vice President Lyndon Johnson. In 1960, Kennedy had chosen him as his running mate. It was a savvy move. Without Johnson delivering the electoral votes of Texas, Kennedy would not have won the election. This would be a major political trip involving private meetings with Democratic leaders, public speeches, and fund-raising events. The president and first lady would visit five cities in two days—San Antonio, Houston, Fort Worth, Dallas, and Austin—and then head to Johnson's Texas ranch to rest. It was an ambitious schedule packed with activities.

In her first campaign trip as first lady, Jacqueline Kennedy would accompany her husband to Texas. She had traveled with JFK to Paris, and without him on private visits to Italy, Greece, India, and Pakistan. But she had not been on a real campaign trip since the presidential election in the fall of 1960. The Texas events would come only three months after her new baby, Patrick Bouvier Kennedy, had died on August 9—two days after he was born.

On November 20, the night before the Kennedys were scheduled to fly to Texas, they hosted an elegant reception in the East Room of the White House for members of the federal judiciary, including the justices of the United States Supreme Court.

The president had received warnings that he might not be entirely welcome in Texas. In Dallas, various political enemies criticized him as either too liberal on civil rights or too soft on Communism. Weeks earlier, the president's opponents had protested a visit to the city by Adlai Stevenson, Kennedy's ambassador to the United Nations. They spat at him, disrupted his

President Kennedy claps his hands as his children, Caroline and John Jr., dance for him in the Oval Office at the White House.

speech, and one woman even hit him in the head with a cardboard sign. In this intemperate political climate, one Kennedy foe printed illustrated handbills, in the style of an Old West wanted poster, to hand out during the Texas trip. It stated that the president was "Wanted for Treason." To ease tensions, the police chief of Dallas planned to go on television to ask his fellow citizens to receive the president with respect.

On the morning of Thursday, November 21, John and Jackie Kennedy said good-bye to their daughter, Caroline, and flew in the presidential helicopter, Marine One, from the White House lawn to Andrews Air Force Base in Maryland. Their son,

John, who was almost three years old, loved flying in the helicopter, so as a special treat they took him along for the ride to Andrews. The boy wanted to fly with his parents to Texas as well. The president told his son that he could not come and that he would see him in a few days. The Kennedys took off from Andrews at 11:05 a.m., flying to Texas on Air Force One, a sleek new jet that had become a symbol of the modern presidency.

John Kennedy had been president of the United States for two years, ten months, and two days. He had left some unfinished paperwork behind on his desk in the Oval Office, including an autographed photograph of himself intended as a gift for a supporter. After inscribing the photo, he had neglected to sign it. It was of no consequence. He could sign his name once he returned from Texas.

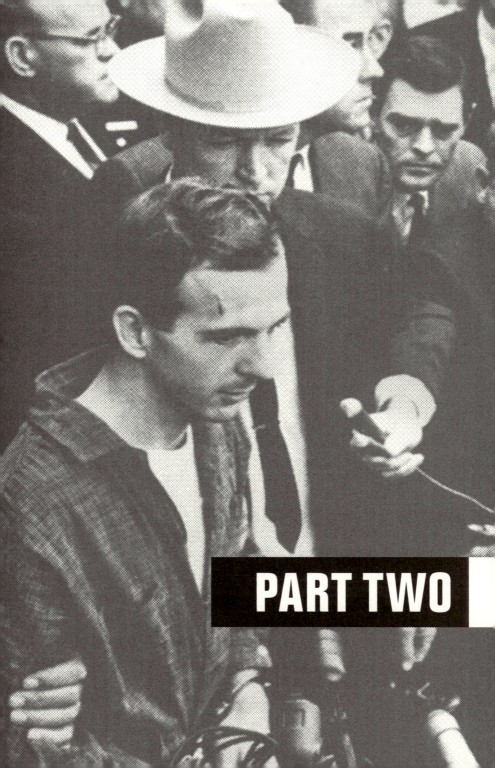

PART TWO

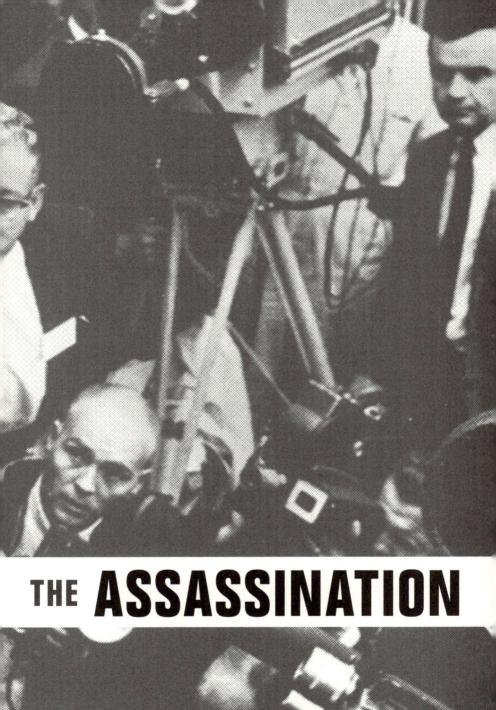

THE ASSASSINATION

THURSDAY
NOVEMBER 21, 1963

The day the Kennedys left the White House for Texas, a man waiting thirteen hundred miles away in Dallas was eager for the president to arrive. He was not an important politician who wanted to discuss business with President Kennedy. He was not a supporter who hoped to shake his hand or to obtain a ticket to the November 22nd Chamber of Commerce breakfast to be held for several hundred people in Fort Worth. He was not attending the lunch planned for more than two thousand people in Dallas. Nor was he a political opponent of John Kennedy's who planned to protest his policies with a homemade, hand-lettered cardboard sign. No, this man who awaited John Kennedy in Texas had something else in mind. He wanted to kill the president.

It was strange. Just two days earlier, when Lee Harvey Oswald awoke in Dallas, Texas, on the morning of Tuesday, November 19, 1963, he did not know that within the next three days he would decide to murder the president of the United States. If a fortune-teller had prophesied his future, the twenty-four-year-old married father of two children might not have believed it. Indeed, among Oswald's corrosive obsessions—and there were many of them—John F. Kennedy was not one. There is no evidence that Oswald hated the president. Much evidence suggests that he rarely thought about him at all. He had no long-standing fixation with Kennedy. He had not made him the primary subject of his everyday conversations. He had not been stalking the president or, as far as can be told, fantasizing about killing him. Of Lee Harvey Oswald's many long-simmering resentments, frustrations, and grievances, the Kennedy presidency was not known to be one of them.

What lured Oswald to his sniper's perch on the afternoon of November 22, 1963, remains one of the most enduring mysteries in modern American history.

On the morning of Tuesday, November 19, the *Dallas Morning News* published the details of the route that President Kennedy's motorcade would follow when, in three days, the presidential jet, Air Force One, would take off from Fort Worth and land in Dallas. On the way to a political fund-raising lunch at the Trade Mart, the presidential limousine, a big, custom-built convertible Lincoln Continental, would travel from the airport — Love Field — through downtown Dallas, allowing thousands of citizens to assemble on the sidewalks and streets to see President Kennedy in person. In addition, many people working in office buildings along the route could open windows overlooking the street to enjoy a good, unobstructed view of the president. After driving through downtown Dallas, the limousine would turn right from Main Street onto Houston Street, proceed one block, then turn left on Elm Street. And, finally, as the crowds thinned in an area known as Dealey Plaza, it would pick up speed, vanish under an overpass, and follow the Stemmons Freeway for a short trip to the Trade Mart lunch. Anyone familiar with the streets of Dallas would know that when the president's car turned left onto Elm, it would pass directly below a seven-story office building and warehouse known as the Texas School Book Depository.

Since mid-October, Lee Harvey Oswald had held a job there as a low-level order filler who moved cardboard boxes of school textbooks around the building. But on the morning of November 19, Oswald probably failed to read that day's newspaper, and he did not learn that in three days John F. Kennedy would drive right past the place he worked. Too cheap to buy a daily paper, Oswald was in the habit of reading stale, day-old newspapers left behind in the lunchroom by coworkers at the Book Depository. Thus, it is likely that it was not until the morning of Wednesday, November 20, two days before President Kennedy was scheduled to arrive in Dallas, that Oswald would have learned for the first time that the president of the United States would drive past the Book Depository.

Oswald must have realized the implications of what he had just read: someone with the mind to do it could open a window on one of the upper stories of the Book Depository, wait for the president's motorcade to drive by, and shoot Kennedy as he passed. The distance between an open window on, say, the fifth, sixth, or seventh floors and Elm Street was too great to fire a pistol at a stationary target below, let alone at a moving car. A pistol's short barrel could not guarantee sufficient accuracy at that range. No, Oswald would have known from his military training, to hit someone from such a distance, he would have to use a rifle.

It had never been attempted before: no American president had ever been assassinated by a rifle. Three of them—Abraham

Lincoln, James Garfield, and William McKinley—had all been murdered at close range—less than two feet—by lone gunmen firing pistols in 1865, 1881, and 1901. And sometimes pistols were not enough. In 1912, former President Theodore Roosevelt had been shot in the chest with a revolver during his campaign for reelection as a third-party candidate, but he survived the wound.

On February 15, 1933, an assassin in Miami, Florida, fired a pistol at a convertible car occupied by president-elect Franklin Roosevelt. The gunman missed his target but wounded the mayor of Chicago, Anton Cermak, who was standing next to Roosevelt's car. Cermak died the next month. And on November 1, 1950, two Puerto Rican nationalists who wanted complete independence from the United States tried to assassinate President Harry Truman by fighting their way with pistols into Blair House, the government guesthouse where he was living during White House renovations. The terrorists shot three policemen, wounding one fatally. One of the assassins was killed, and the other was captured. The gunmen never got into the president's residence.

Four years later, on March 1, 1954, while Congress was in session, a gang of four other Puerto Rican nationalists sitting in the visitor's gallery of the House of Representatives opened fire with semiautomatic pistols, wounding, but not killing, five congressmen. To this day, bullet holes from the attack scar the furniture in the House chamber. No, a pistol was not a foolproof weapon for an assassination.

What brought John Kennedy and Lee Harvey Oswald

together was a staggering coincidence. It is likely that Oswald would never have thought of killing Kennedy at all if the publicized motorcade route had not taken JFK to the doorstep of Oswald's place of employment. It was a once-in-a-lifetime opportunity — the president was coming to him! Oswald thought about it. He possessed the necessary skill and equipment. He had learned to shoot in the U.S. Marine Corps, and he owned a rifle. He could do it. Yes, he could. But would he? And why?

Oswald had always wanted to star in a historic moment. He was born in New Orleans, Louisiana, in October 1939, the youngest of three brothers. But a dark cloud formed over him even before he entered the world. His father died two months before he was born, and during his unsettled childhood, his odd and unstable mother changed husbands, houses, jobs, and cities frequently — often turning over the care of her boys to orphanages or relatives. When Lee was growing up, he lived, among other places, in New Orleans, Fort Worth, Manhattan and the Bronx in New York City, and then New Orleans and Fort Worth again. Young Lee had disciplinary problems at school, made few friends, threatened family members with knives, rebelled against any kind of authority, and missed so much school that he was tracked down by truant officers and ordered to appear at court hearings.

Oswald exhibited an interest in the Soviet Union and the teachings of Socialism, Marxism, and Communism. These were strange pursuits for an American teenage boy during the middle of the Cold War, an era in which the United States and the Soviet

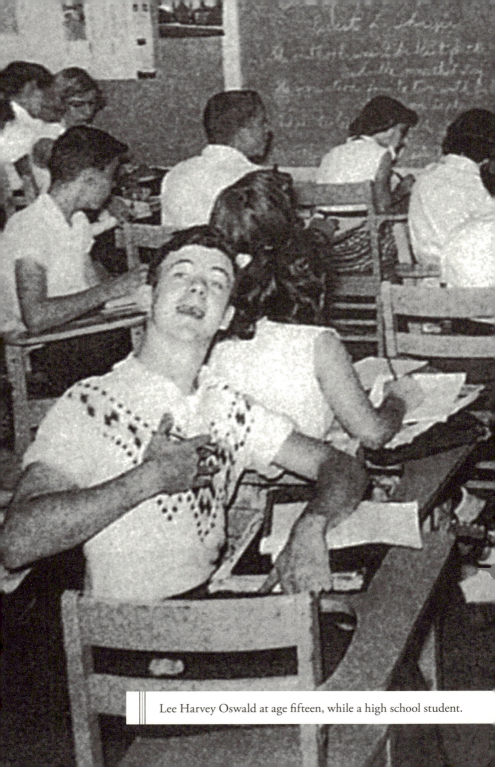

Lee Harvey Oswald at age fifteen, while a high school student.

Union were locked in an intense ideological battle, and being a Communist in America could trigger a government investigation.

In September 1956, Oswald dropped out of high school altogether. And in October, after he turned seventeen, he enlisted in the United States Marine Corps. He served at bases in America and Japan, where he was court-martialed twice: once for assaulting a superior, and once for accidentally shooting himself in the arm with a Deringer pistol — the same type of single-shot weapon that John Wilkes Booth used to murder Abraham Lincoln.

When Oswald was stationed in Taiwan, he suffered a nervous breakdown and had to be transferred to Japan for medical reasons. Throughout his three years in the Marine Corps, Oswald was a malcontent and constant complainer who loved to argue with his superiors to show that he was smarter than they were. He also made no secret of his interest in Communist societies. He received no better than average performance ratings, but the Marine Corps managed to teach him to do one thing well — shoot a rifle with skill and reasonable accuracy.

In September 1959, under false pretenses, he requested a dependency discharge to care for his mother. Oswald was granted his discharge. Then, in October 1959, in a series of bizarre events, he traveled to the Soviet Union, showed up in Moscow, and tried to commit suicide when his visa (the document permitting him to visit the Soviet Union) expired and he was ordered to leave the country. He then went to the United States embassy in an attempt to renounce his American citizenship. Soviet officials, though suspicious that he might be mentally unstable, allowed Oswald to remain in the country, and assigned him a job at a radio factory. In April 1961, he married a nineteen-year-old Russian woman named Marina Prusakova. After a few years, Oswald grew dissatisfied with life in Russia, and he wanted to return to the United States. He was no longer the exotic foreigner and center of attention that he had been when he had first defected. He, Marina, and their infant

Lee Harvey Oswald with his wife, Marina, and their first daughter, June.

daughter left the Soviet Union in June 1962 and traveled to Fort Worth, Texas, where his mother and brother lived.

On January 28, 1963, Oswald purchased a .38 caliber Smith & Wesson revolver by mail order. On March 12, 1963, he mail-ordered a surplus World War II Italian rifle, a 6.5 mm, bolt-action Mannlicher-Carcano mounted with a telescopic sight. He paid for both items using a false name. On March 25, the two weapons arrived at his post office box, which he had also obtained under a false name. Later, he had his wife take photographs of him in the backyard holding his new rifle and wearing the pistol on his belt. On April 1, Oswald, who could never hold a job for long, was fired from his most recent one. April 6 was his last day at work, and on April 10 he crossed the line from malcontent to madman. That night, Oswald attempted to assassinate former U.S. Army General Edwin Walker.

Walker led the local chapter of the John Birch Society, an energetic and vocal anti-Communist private organization named after an American who had been killed by Chinese Communists. Walker was also an outspoken opponent of school desegregation and President Kennedy. Oswald had stalked Walker and, just a few weeks earlier, had spied on and photographed his house. On the night of April 10, Oswald went to Walker's home. Through a window, Oswald could see the general in a well-lit room. He was the perfect target. Oswald aimed his rifle at Walker's head and fired. But he missed. Too afraid to fire another shot, he concealed his rifle in the vicinity and ran off into the dark. He didn't want to get caught with the weapon in his possession on his way home. Shortly after that, Oswald came back and retrieved his rifle from its hiding place. The attack on General

Lee Harvey Oswald poses with his rifle and pistol.

Walker was a turning point for Oswald: it was the first time he had ever tried to kill a man.

Soon after that, Oswald decided to leave Texas and moved to New Orleans. In late May, he wrote to an obscure organization called the Fair Play for Cuba Committee (FPCC). It was a group that lobbied for fair treatment of the island nation after its revolutionary dictator, Fidel Castro, had installed a Communist government there. By June, he was distributing FPCC handbills on the streets of New Orleans. In July, he was fired from yet another job, and the U.S. Navy (which had jurisdiction over the Marine Corps) affirmed its decision to change his discharge from the Marine Corps to undesirable after it learned that he had tried to defect to the Soviet Union. In letters to Secretary of the Navy John Connally, Oswald had argued, without success, that the service should reinstate the honorable discharge he had been given when he left the marines, before he moved to Russia.

In August 1963, Oswald was arrested after a street brawl with Cuban anti-Communists who objected to his distribution of pro-Castro literature. The incident attracted the notice of the press, and on August 17 and August 21, Lee Harvey Oswald participated in two New Orleans radio shows to discuss Cuba, Communism, and Marxism. The host of the program surprised him by exposing his defection to Russia, so Oswald was compelled to also discuss his life there. Nonetheless, he enjoyed his notoriety and the public attention he had received.

By the fall, Lee's wife, Marina, was fed up with life in New Orleans and with her husband. Lee had become short-tempered and violent, and on several occasions he had hit or beaten her.

Oswald distributes "Hands off Cuba" flyers in New Orleans in the summer of 1963, when he was a member of the Fair Play for Cuba Committee.

He had also confessed to her the Walker assassination attempt, which had terrified her.

On September 23, 1963, Marina left New Orleans for Irving, Texas, a suburb of Dallas. She was expecting their second child next month, and her friend Ruth Paine had offered to take her in and care for her. Lee left New Orleans too, and four days later, on September 27, he showed up in Mexico City, where he visited the Cuban embassy and applied for permission to travel there. The Cubans gave him no special treatment and told him it would take months. Frustrated, he then went to the Russian embassy for help in getting to Cuba or returning to the Soviet Union. The Russians knew he was an odd duck and were in no hurry to allow him back into their country either. He was furious.

Oswald returned to the United States and on October 3 showed up in Dallas, where he visited Marina at Ruth Paine's house in Irving and spent the weekend of October 12–14 there. Paine worried that Oswald was having trouble getting a job, and she told some of her friends that he needed work. On the night of October 14, after Lee had returned to Dallas, Ruth told him over the phone that a girlfriend of hers said they were hiring at a place called the Texas School Book Depository. Oswald applied in person the next day. He was hired and started work on October 16. He and Marina agreed that he would live at a rooming house in Dallas during the week and visit Marina at Ruth Paine's house in Irving on the weekends. Ruth, who disliked Lee and hated the way he treated his wife, hoped that Marina would leave him. A neighbor of Ruth's, Buell Wesley Frazier, also worked at the Book Depository, and he offered to drive Oswald from Dallas to Irving on Fridays after work and back to the Book Depository on Monday mornings. Marina threw her husband a surprise birthday party that week, and he seemed touched. Then, on October 20, 1963, their new baby daughter was born. Perhaps Oswald's odd and unsettled life would finally calm down.

On October 23, Lee attended a right-wing political rally where General Walker spoke. Was this a warning sign that he was plotting another assassination attempt? Then the Federal Bureau of Investigation (FBI) made a couple of visits to Marina Oswald. They told her they would like to speak to Lee. It was nothing serious, just a follow-up to chat with him since he returned home from Russia almost seventeen months ago. The visits angered Oswald — he believed that the FBI agents were harassing Marina. On November 12, he left an angry note at the

FBI headquarters in Dallas for agent James Hosty, telling him to leave his family alone.

Who *was* this strange man named Lee Harvey Oswald? In the fall of 1963, he was a lifelong loser, a high school dropout, a second-rate ex–U.S. Marine, and a malcontent with a chip on his shoulder. On November 19, Lee Oswald was a complaining, self-pitying, attention-seeking, temperamental, impoverished ideologue, and a man of slight build with an oversize ego. Despite his long record of incompetence at even menial jobs, he believed himself superior to others, and he despised authority. He had always dreamed of big things, but he'd failed at everything he had ever attempted. He was still a young man — he had just turned twenty-four — but was living a dead-end life of unskilled, low-paying jobs and humiliation by superiors, with an inability to provide for his family. He was insignificant. He wanted to stand out. Oswald had delusions of grandeur, and he dreamed of accomplishing great things. But in reality, he was the feckless father of two young children whom he could barely afford to feed and clothe. He was the bad husband of a wife he insulted and abused. He could not control events. He could not even control his own life. His marriage had failed, his prospects for a better life were failing, and his life as a whole was a failure.

He claimed he was a Marxist and pretended to be an intellectual, but he persuaded no one of his intelligence or wit. All he could muster were humorless slogans and theories he had memorized from books and political tracts. Was he a true believer and supporter of Communist principles and dictatorships? Or was this all a fraudulent pose he adopted in adolescence to be different, to stand out from the crowd, to gain attention?

Sometime over the next three days, between the morning of November 19 and the afternoon of November 21, Lee Harvey Oswald would decide to assassinate President Kennedy. No one knows exactly when he made that decision. It could have been as early as the morning of Tuesday, November 19, but only if he broke his habit and read the morning paper the same day it came out. If he followed his usual custom, then he would not have read Tuesday's paper until the following day, the morning of November 20. Once Oswald read the day-old paper, perhaps he also consulted Wednesday's *Dallas Times Herald*, the afternoon paper, which confirmed the motorcade route. Then, on Thursday, November 21, to make sure that the public knew where to go to see the president, the morning paper published a map of the route that Kennedy's motorcade would follow.

A deviation from Oswald's normal behavior offers an intriguing clue. On the morning of November 21, he ate breakfast at the Dobbs House restaurant. He was not in the habit of buying breakfast, and he did not have the money to do it. Did breaking his routine by treating himself to a special breakfast signal that something was different and that he had decided by the morning of the twenty-first to assassinate the president? No one will ever know.

Depending on the exact timing of his decision, Oswald had about twenty to fifty hours to make — and carry out — his scheme. He was a trained and experienced rifleman who would have known that a successful assassination required careful

The Texas School Book Depository is easily identified by the Hertz sign and the digital clock on the roof. Oswald's window is on the sixth floor on the far right column of windows.

advance planning. He could not just poke his rifle out of a random Book Depository window on November 22, and start shooting away, hoping to hit his target. No, a sniper attack combined angles, timing, stealth, concealment, and patience. And an escape route. Oswald could not leave these details until the last minute.

Where, Oswald might have asked himself, was the best location in the Texas School Book Depository from which to carry out the shooting? One of the upper floors, high over the street, would place him above the sight lines of parade watchers and the passengers in the multicar motorcade. He could position himself to shoot down at the president, from an angle that would make it difficult for witnesses to spot him. Oswald chose the sixth floor.

To accommodate construction work that involved replacing

This aerial view of Dealey Plaza shows the Texas School Book Depository on the left, with the Hertz sign and the digital clock on the roof.

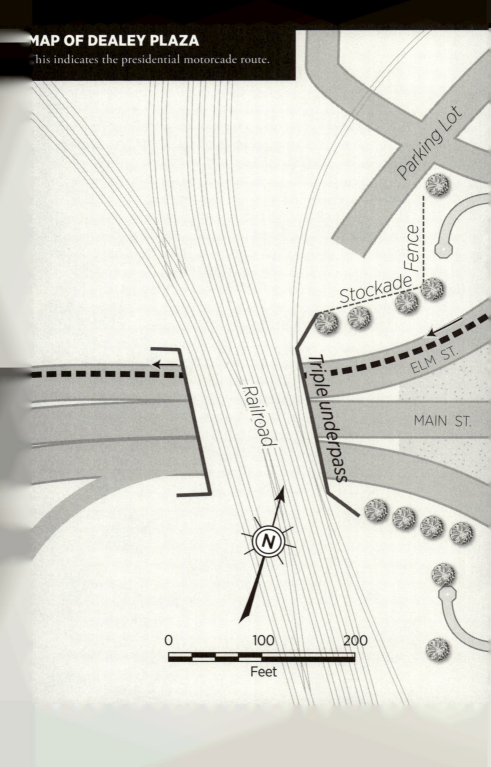

Parking Lot

Stockade Fence

ELM ST.

Triple underpass

MAIN ST.

Railroad

N

0   100   200
Feet

Texas School Book Depository

Dal-Tex Building

ELM ST.

County Records Building

County Criminal Courts Building

Reflecting Pool

HOUSTON ST.

RECORD ST.

DEALEY PLAZA

Presidential motorcade route

Old Court House

John Neely Bryan House

Women's Recreation Hall

CE ST.

COMMERCE ST.

a portion of the wooden flooring, workers had moved many heavy cardboard cartons full of books to the south side of the floor, near the row of windows looking down upon Elm Street. There were twice as many boxes on that side of the building as normal. Stacks of them obstructed a clear sight line across the room and would shield anyone who wanted to remain hidden from the view of anyone else on that floor. It would be as easy as a child stacking building blocks to move some of those cartons and arrange them into a wall on November 22. He could set up his position at the window of his choice. He could even shift a couple of boxes to the edge of the windowsill and rest his rifle on the top one to steady his aim. Yes, the layout and current condition of the sixth floor was perfect for an assassin.

The large number of boxes on the floor would also make it easy for Oswald to stash his weapon. He would need to hide the rifle from other Book Depository workers for four hours, between the time he brought it to work around 8:00 a.m. until around noon, when he would retrieve it. Then he would take his position behind the boxes and wait for his prey.

After the deed was done, Oswald planned to leave the rifle behind at the Book Depository. There was almost no chance that he could descend five flights of stairs or take the elevator with a rifle in his hands without encountering coworkers, or any policemen or Secret Service agents who might storm the building after they heard the shots. Even if Oswald escaped the Book Depository, he could hardly expect to stroll unnoticed down Elm Street with a rifle slung over his shoulder. He could try to disassemble it on the sixth floor and stuff it into the same brown paper bag he would use to carry it to the office that morning,

Inside the Texas School Book Depository looking toward Oswald's sixth-floor window.

but that procedure would cost too much time. Every second would be precious to Oswald's escape. No, he would have to abandon his weapon on the sixth floor.

No criminal wants to leave a murder weapon behind at the scene of the crime. A firearm is an incriminating piece of evidence. It can bear fingerprints that identify a gunman. Firearms possess serial numbers that can be traced. The inside grooves of a rifle barrel leave unique marks on a bullet so that a spent round can be identified later as having been fired from that weapon. A brass cartridge case ejected from a rifle after the bullet has been fired can bear telltale signs that match it to the weapon from which it came. It would be risky for Oswald to leave his rifle at the Book Depository. Though he had purchased it by mail under a false name and had it shipped to a post office box—not his home address—there was still a chance that law enforcement officials could trace it to him. But carrying a rifle out the front door was sure to be even more dangerous.

The would-be assassin had chosen his floor and his method of disposing of the rifle. Now he had to pick his window. Fourteen large, tall double-hung windows ran along the south wall facing Elm Street. President Kennedy would ride past all of them. Oswald had a choice of any of them from which to aim his rifle. He selected one, the window at the far southeast corner. At some point he might have rehearsed his plans, performing a walk-through of the assassination. Perhaps he walked the length of the wall, peering down to Elm Street through each window, assessing the suitability of its angle of view.

At the last window on the left, Oswald must have noticed its two advantages over all the other windows on the floor. First,

Oswald's perch inside the Book Depository, overlooking Dealey Plaza.

it looked straight down Houston Street, the route that Kennedy's limousine would follow to Elm Street on November 22. As Oswald watched the traffic come up Houston Street, he could not have avoided noticing what a perfect target any car on that road would be.

The president would follow that identical route. In other words, for one block, the president would drive directly toward the Depository, up Houston Street, and toward that window. From Kennedy's point of view, the window was the one on the far right end of the sixth floor. From Oswald's perspective, he would have an unobstructed, head-on view of the president's car as it drove closer and closer toward the Book Depository.

Then, right below the Depository, the president's car would slow almost to a stop to make the hairpin, tight-angled left turn onto Elm Street. From almost the moment that the car made the turn and then continued along the length of the Book Depository, anyone standing in that window would have, for at least ten or fifteen seconds, a perfect view of the back of the presidential limousine. That was plenty of time to get off two to four well-aimed shots. No other window on the sixth floor offered an earlier or longer look at the back of the car. Here, Oswald decided, he would build his sniper's nest.

By the afternoon of Thursday, November 21, Oswald was willing but not yet equipped to carry out the assassination the next day. He needed his rifle. But it was not in his possession. Oswald and his estranged wife, Marina, had been living apart on weekdays. He kept small quarters at a Dallas rooming house at 1026 North Beckley Avenue, and that is where he kept his .38 caliber snub-nosed revolver designed for concealment.

Police-style revolvers, unlike Oswald's, had longer barrels, which made them more accurate but harder to hide from view.

If Oswald wanted to use his short-barreled weapon for the assassination, he could never do it from the sixth-floor window. Instead, he would have to do it from close range at Love Field, where Air Force One was scheduled to land at about noon on November 22. There Oswald would have to merge into the crowd that had assembled to greet the president — there were sure to be some hecklers, possibly even holding unflattering signs or waving Confederate flags — and work his way to the front of the throng. Then, as the president shook hands with well-wishers, Oswald could extend his arm and, instead of shaking hands, shoot Kennedy with his six-shot revolver. It would be a risky move, with no guarantee of success. Whenever President Kennedy interacted with the public in close quarters, one or two Secret Service agents armed with pistols stood by his side, watching the crowd. Even if Oswald succeeded, he could have never escaped the scene. This was not a suicide mission — it was not part of his plan to trade his life for the president's.

He would need to get his rifle that he kept at the home of Mrs. Ruth Paine, the woman who had befriended his wife and taken her in. Oswald had stored it in Paine's garage. And, on the evening of November 21, it still lay on the floor of that crowded room, wrapped in a blanket and hidden from view. Oswald had to get that rifle. But it was a Thursday, not a Friday. He was not supposed to drop in at Ruth Paine's unannounced. He had never gone to Irving on a weekday. Tonight, he would have to make an exception to that rule. Lee, who did not own a car or have a driver's license, caught a ride with Buell Wesley Frazier.

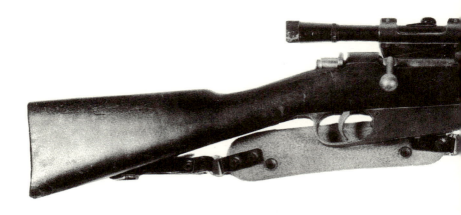

Marina was surprised, and not too happy, to see her quarrelsome, violent husband. Then Ruth Paine came home after shopping for groceries. She had never liked Lee, and was even less pleased to find him at her home on a day he was not supposed to be there. Oswald's visit was a pretext to go into her garage and retrieve his Mannlicher-Carcano. He planned to spend Thursday night in Irving and then on Friday morning bring it to work.

Perhaps it was the sight of his attractive young wife, his two-year-old daughter, and his newborn baby girl that seemed to have softened his murderous heart. Maybe he would not kill President Kennedy the next day after all. He spoke kind words uncharacteristic of a killer.

Lee told Marina that he loved her and asked her to move back to Dallas and live with him there. She said no. He said he would rent a nice apartment for them and the children where they could begin their lives anew. She refused. He offered to buy her a new washing machine — it was hard for her to keep up with the laundry for two small children. If Oswald was not thinking about changing his mind about killing Kennedy, he

The Mannlicher-Carcano rifle that Oswald purchased and used to assassinate President Kennedy. This was also the same rifle Oswald used in his failed attempt on General Walker's life.

would have had no reason to find a better apartment, or purchase a washing machine. Marina told Lee to spend the money on something for himself. Lee went to bed before her and turned off the light. But when Marina joined him, she sensed that he was still awake, only pretending to be asleep. And when she, in a gesture of intimacy in the darkness of the night, extended her leg to touch his, he kicked it away.

As the night lengthened on November 21, 1963, Lee Harvey Oswald could not escape the hopelessness of his life. He was a lonely, impoverished, and embittered young man who had failed at everything in life that he had ever attempted — high school, the Marine Corps, marriage, fatherhood, menial jobs, political activism, writing, being an expatriate, and significance. And now, on this night, he had failed in love. He was helpless, drifting toward oblivion. Tomorrow he would change that.

Sometime that night, no one knows exactly when, Oswald walked into the garage, turned on the light, and lifted up the blanket and its deadly contents. The Mannlicher-Carcano was still there. Marina hated that rifle, and she had thought more than once about disposing of it. She never forgot the day, not

Evidence seized after the assassination: the blanket used to conceal the rifle in Mrs. Paine's garage, the brown paper bag in which Oswald concealed the rifle on his way to work, and the rifle disassembled to show how Oswald carried it to work on the morning of November 22.

long after he bought it, that Lee made her photograph him holding it and wearing his pistol on his belt. She also remembered when he confessed to her that he had taken a shot at General Walker. He had promised not to shoot at anyone again. That night, in addition to his rifle, Lee realized he also needed ammunition. He had depleted his supply at a target range. All he had left in his possession were four bullets. These would have to be enough. He disassembled the weapon and slipped the pieces into a bag he had made with brown paper and tape at the Book Depository. Later that night, probably not until long after midnight, Lee Harvey Oswald drifted off to sleep.

FRIDAY
NOVEMBER 22, 1963

On the morning of November 22, Lee woke up early and was out of bed before Marina. He told her not to get up. He went to the kitchen and served himself a cup of coffee. Marina did not see what he did next. On top of the dresser he left her $170 in cash, almost all the money he had. And in a porcelain cup that she had brought with her all the way from Russia, Lee Oswald left his wedding ring. He told Marina he would not be back tonight. Sleeping on the idea had not changed his mind. He left the house, went into the garage, and emerged with his package. He walked to the nearby home of Buell Wesley Frazier, his coworker from the Book Depository. By prearrangement, Frazier had offered to give Lee a ride to work that day. Oswald's package caught the man's eye.

"What's in the bag?" he asked Lee.

"Curtain rods," replied Oswald, as he tossed his package onto the backseat. Then the men got into the car and drove to Dallas.

• • •

At the same time Lee Harvey Oswald was driving to work, John and Jacqueline Kennedy were awake in their suite at the Hotel Texas in Fort Worth. The president dressed first. He was scheduled to go downstairs and deliver brief remarks to a crowd that had assembled in a parking lot across the street. He looked outside. It was a gloomy, rainy day. The Secret Service worried about the weather in Dallas. The president's limousine had already been sent there ahead of Kennedy, so it would be in position when he landed at Love Field. The car was a convertible, and the agents wondered if they should install the plastic bubble top to protect the president from the rain. John Kennedy preferred to ride in an open car so the people watching the motorcade could get a better look at him. It created an intimacy with the crowd. Jackie did not like the open car — the wind would play havoc with her stylish hair.

While in Fort Worth, Kennedy would travel in a rented convertible. It was unarmored. If a madman jumped from the curb and fired shots, the bullets could penetrate the metal doors of the car. During Kennedy's trip to Berlin, two women had broken through the security cordon and had run right up to his car in a motorcade. They turned out to be overenthusiastic but harmless fans.

This morning in his hotel room, John Kennedy saw in the newspaper a full-page ad that made him wonder how many such madmen might be out there. At first glance, the boldfaced headline, WELCOME MR. KENNEDY TO DALLAS, seemed to be a friendly greeting. But as he read further, the president saw a long list of complaints attacking him and his administration. The ad irked him. "We're heading into nut country today," he told Jackie.

Then, before he left the room, he said an eerie thing to his wife: "You know, last night would have been a hell of a night to assassinate a president. There was the rain, and the night, and

WELCOME MR. KENNEDY

TO DALLAS...

...A CITY so disgraced by a recent Liberal smear attempt that its citizens have just elected two more Conservative Americans to public office.

...A CITY that is an economic "boom town," not because of Federal handouts, but through conservative economic and business practices.

...A CITY that will continue to grow and prosper despite efforts by you and your administration to penalize it for its non-conformity to New Frontierism.

...A CITY that rejected your philosophy and policies in 1960 and will do so again in 1964—even more emphatically than before.

MR. KENNEDY, despite contentions on the part of your administration, the State Department, the Mayor of Dallas, the Dallas City Council, and members of your party, we free-thinking and America-thinking citizens of Dallas still have, through a Constitution largely ignored by you, the right to address our grievances, to question you, to disagree with you, and to criticize you.

In asserting this constitutional right, we wish to ask you publicly the following questions—indeed, questions of paramount importance and interest to all free peoples everywhere—which we trust you will answer . . . in public, without sophistry. These questions are:

WHY is Latin America turning either anti-American or Communistic, or both, despite increased U. S. foreign aid, State Department policy, and your own Ivy-Tower pronouncements?

WHY do you say we have built a "wall of freedom" around Cuba when there is no freedom in Cuba today? Because of your policy, thousands of Cubans have been imprisoned, are starving and being persecuted—with thousands already murdered and thousands more awaiting execution and, in addition, the entire population of almost 7,000,000 Cubans are living in slavery.

WHY have you approved the sale of wheat and corn to our enemies when you know the Communist soldiers "travel on their stomachs" just as ours do? Communist soldiers are daily wounding and or killing American soldiers in South Viet Nam.

WHY did you host, salute and entertain Tito — Moscow's Trojan Horse — just a short time after our sworn enemy, Khrushchev, embraced the Yugoslav dictator as a great hero and leader of Communism?

WHY have you urged greater aid, comfort, recognition, and understanding for Yugoslavia, Poland, Hungary, and other Communist countries, while turning your back on the pleas of Hungarian, East German, Cuban and other anti-Communist freedom fighters?

WHY did Cambodia kick the U.S. out of its country after we poured nearly 400 Million Dollars of aid into its ultra-leftist government?

WHY has Gus Hall, head of the U.S. Communist Party praised almost every one of your policies and announced that the party will endorse and support your re-election in 1964?

WHY have you banned the showing at U.S. military bases of the film "Operation Abolition"—the movie by the House Committee on Un-American Activities exposing Communism in America?

WHY have you ordered or permitted your brother Bobby, the Attorney General, to go soft on Communists, fellow-travelers, and ultra-leftists in America, while permitting him to persecute loyal Americans who criticize you, your administration, and your leadership?

WHY are you in favor of the U.S. continuing to give economic aid to Argentina, in spite of that fact that Argentina has just seized almost 400 Million Dollars of American private property?

WHY has the Foreign Policy of the United States degenerated to the point that the C.I.A. is arranging coups and having staunch Anti-Communist Allies of the U.S. bloodily exterminated.

WHY have you scrapped the Monroe Doctrine in favor of the "Spirit of Moscow"?

MR. KENNEDY, as citizens of these United States of America, we DEMAND answers to these questions, and we want them NOW.

THE AMERICAN FACT-FINDING COMMITTEE

"An unaffiliated and non-partisan group of citizens who wish truth"

BERNARD WEISSMAN,
Chairman

P.O. Box 1792 — Dallas 21, Texas

The anti-Kennedy statement that appeared in the *Dallas Morning News*

we were all getting jostled. Suppose a man had a pistol in a briefcase and melted away into the crowd?"

Perhaps the president recalled a letter he wrote in 1959, the year before the election. Kennedy replied to a man who had written to him about the "thought-provoking . . . historical curiosity" that since 1840 every man who entered the White House in a year ending in zero had not left the White House alive. JFK replied that "the future will necessarily answer" what his fate will be should he have "the privilege of occupying the White House."

Kennedy went downstairs to speak at 8:45 a.m. (CST) to the cheering crowd outside standing in the rain. "There are no faint hearts in Fort Worth, and I appreciate your being here this morning." Then, to explain Jackie's absence, he joked with the crowd: "Mrs. Kennedy is organizing herself. It takes longer, but, of course, she looks better than we do when she does it."

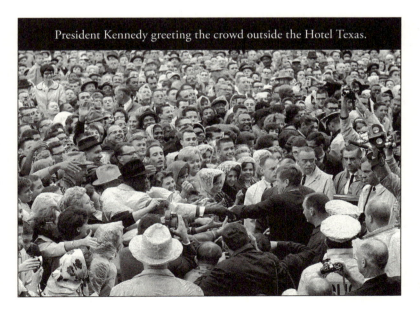
President Kennedy greeting the crowd outside the Hotel Texas.

On the morning of November 22, Kennedy addresses the crowd outside the Hotel Texas in Forth Worth. One block away, open windows offer an unobstructed view of the president.

Back in their hotel room, as Jackie got dressed, she heard his voice over the loudspeakers. She could not know it was the last time he would ever address a spontaneous gathering of American citizens.

The president returned to the hotel at 9:00 a.m. to speak at a public breakfast in the ballroom. But Jackie's seat at the head table was empty. The disappointed guests wanted to see her. Kennedy told one of his Secret Service agents to call Jackie's room and tell her to get down to the breakfast as soon as possible.

JFK stalled for time: "Two years ago, I introduced myself in Paris by saying that I was the man who had accompanied Mrs. Kennedy to Paris. I am getting somewhat that same sensation as I travel around Texas. Nobody wonders what Lyndon and I wear."

Then a commotion began at the back of the room. Jackie had arrived, and the crowd shouted its approval. She did not disappoint. She was wearing a bright pink, nubby wool jacket (Jackie called the color raspberry), faced with dark blue lapels and a matching pink skirt, and a pink pillbox hat. She wore bright white cotton gloves, a fashionable accessory for women at that time. It was one of the most flattering outfits in her wardrobe, and she had worn it on several prior occasions. The colorful suit seemed almost to glow, and created a striking contrast against her rich black hair and pale white skin. She looked radiant. Fashion and movie magazines covered Jackie as a style-setter, and the president was aware of how her beauty and elegant fashion sense were priceless political assets that further enhanced his popularity.

• • •

Meanwhile, at around 7:52 a.m., Lee Oswald and Wesley Frazier, as he liked to be called, arrived at the outdoor parking lot several hundred feet behind the Texas School Book Depository. Oswald jumped out of the car, reached into the backseat for his package of "curtain rods," and walked fast toward the Depository, getting as far ahead of Frazier as he could without breaking into a run. He opened the back door and slipped inside. Then he ascended to the sixth floor, using either the staircase at the back of the building or one of the freight elevators. He probably took the stairs to avoid riding an elevator with any curious coworkers who might ask questions about his package.

Once he was sure that no one was watching him, he hid the package containing the still-unassembled rifle between stacks of book boxes on the sixth floor. It is possible that he assembled the rifle that morning before hiding it, in case later unforeseeable circumstances prevented him from doing so during the critical moments before Kennedy's motorcade arrived. No one knows for sure. With his rifle concealed from view, Oswald picked up his clipboard and began filling orders for books, just as he did on any other normal day in the office. At least until the presidential motorcade approached Elm Street, Oswald would, for the next three hours, earn his pay.

• • •

In Fort Worth, President Kennedy's motorcade left the Hotel Texas for Carswell Air Force Base. It would be a short flight — just thirteen minutes — to Dallas. They took off at 11:25 a.m. (CST). Air Force One landed at Love Field in Dallas at 11:38 a.m. It was an hour later in the nation's capital, and most officials in Washington were at lunch. Several members of the cabinet were out of the country, aboard a plane flying to Japan for meetings with government officials.

• • •

At the Texas School Book Depository, lunch hour would soon begin. Most of the employees would start their noontime descent from the upper floors to congregate in the lunchroom on the second floor, or to go outside and watch President Kennedy drive by on Elm Street. The biggest crowds to see the president had already gathered downtown, choking the sidewalks several people deep before JFK had even landed. Hundreds of people perched in windows looked down on the route. The Secret Service and the Dallas police did not have the manpower — or the desire — to search every building, to scrutinize every window, or to analyze every face. It was impossible.

But there, in Dealey Plaza, where the motorcade would reach the last leg of its ten-mile route before it picked up speed and took the highway to the Trade Mart, the crowds were much thinner. It was easy for the scattered spectators to stake out a spot right at the edge of the curb and stand just a few feet away from where the president's limousine would soon pass. Indeed, people standing on the right side of the car would be closest to Kennedy, in some cases less than six feet from him. Things were much calmer and quieter in Dealey Plaza, in the vicinity of the Texas School Book Depository, than they were downtown.

• • •

At Love Field, the president and first lady exited the door of Air Force One and descended the portable stairs that airport workers had rolled out to the plane. Waiting for them on the ground

In Dallas, Jackie and JFK disembark from Air Force One.

were a number of local dignitaries and politicians, including Vice President Lyndon B. Johnson, who had flown to Dallas ahead of the Kennedys. Protocol dictated that LBJ, a Texan, would welcome the president at each stop within the state.

The wife of the mayor presented Jackie with a big bouquet of flowers. The yellow rose was the official state flower, but so many of them had been ordered for the various events the

The Kennedys at Love Field in Dallas. Jackie has just been presented a bouquet of red roses.

Kennedys would attend in Texas that local florists had run out of them. Instead, the mayor's wife had handed Jackie a bouquet of red roses. The deep crimson petals looked striking against her pink suit.

After greeting the airport reception committee, the president noticed that a few thousand people standing behind a chain-link fence had turned up at Love Field to see him. Some carried flags and signs, most of which were friendly. Someone brought a Confederate battle flag, a possible sign of protest against the president. JFK, who treated the whole Texas trip like a campaign stop in preparation for the November 1964 election, made an impulsive decision to work the fence line. Jackie, cradling the red roses, followed him. At that moment, a news photographer named Art Rickerby, who had gotten ahead of the Kennedys, took a series of color photographs of the couple as they walked side by side. The president's medium blue suit and tie, and Jackie's bright pink suit and red roses, saturated the camera's color film. Behind them was the big red, white, and blue American flag painted on the tail of Air Force One. When the people in the crowd realized that the president of the United States was coming over to visit them, they went wild.

Kennedy walked right up to them and plunged his arms over the hip-high fence. Hundreds of hands grabbed his. As Jackie walked the line, women begged to touch her and squealed with delight if they succeeded. The limousine crawled along behind the president. After JFK shook a last hand, he and Jackie turned to the limousine. The bubble top was off. They would ride through Dallas in an open car. Earlier that morning, the agents gambled that the gray skies and rain would disappear by

Jackie and JFK greet well-wishers along the fence line shortly after their arrival at Dallas.

noon. Their bet paid off. It was a bright, gorgeous, and sunny fall day.

The president sat in the right rear passenger seat. Jackie took her seat to his left. In front of the Kennedys, sitting at a slightly lower level in folding jump seats that also faced forward, were the governor of Texas, John Connally, and his wife, Nellie. In the front seat sat the driver and the head of the Secret Service detail. Behind the president's car was another convertible filled with Secret Service agents. Following behind them were several other vehicles, whose passengers included Vice President Johnson and his wife, Lady Bird, several Texas politicians, members of the press, and White House staff, including the president's

personal secretary, Evelyn Lincoln. As the motorcade got under way, led by police motorcycles and a white car carrying the Dallas chief of police, Jesse Curry, someone filmed the Kennedy's departure from Love Field until their limousine vanished from sight. They were scheduled to arrive at the Trade Mart lunch by 12:30 p.m. JFK's spontaneous visit with the airport crowd had put him a little behind schedule. If the motorcade experienced no more delays, they would arrive at their lunch by about 12:35 p.m.

• • •

Back in Dealey Plaza, the electric digital clock on the big yellow Hertz-Rent-a-Car sign atop the Depository roof flashed the time. It was past noon. As Lee Oswald's coworkers came down for lunch, he proceeded to the sixth floor. A few asked him if he was having lunch or whether he planned to watch the president with them. He lingered and gave vague answers. According to what the newspapers said, Kennedy's car should have been in front of the Depository by about 12:15 or 12:20 p.m.

Lee Harvey Oswald was now alone on the sixth floor. He retrieved his rifle, either in pieces from inside the brown paper bag or already fully assembled. He walked to the southeast corner of the building and took his position at the window. If the lower pane was not already open, he slid it up now and secured it in position. He inhaled the fresh, crisp fall air. It was about sixty-five degrees. If he had looked down Houston Street, he would have heard no sounds nor seen any signs that the motorcade was near. No police motorcycles were in sight yet, and people on the street were not fidgeting or craning their necks the way excited crowds do when a president of the United States is approaching. Perhaps Lee adjusted some of the boxes to ensure that no one who came up to this floor could see him as he hid behind them. He still had a few minutes. He checked his rifle. It was ready to fire. One round was already in the chamber. Three more rounds waited in the clip, if Oswald needed to use them. If he heeded the warnings drilled into him by his Marine Corps training, he would have switched on the safety mechanism of his rifle. That device would prevent the weapon from firing a round accidentally if the shooter dropped and jarred it, or snagged the trigger. As long as the safety was engaged, squeezing the trigger would fail to release the firing pin, and the rifle could not fire the chambered round. Once the president came within sight, Oswald could, by disabling the safety with the flick of a thumb, render his weapon lethal in an instant. He waited in silence. The only sounds were the occasional voices that floated up from the street below before they faded into nothingness.

• • •

Minute by minute, President Kennedy's motorcade drew closer to the Book Depository. The journey through downtown Dallas was more of a parade than a motorcade. On the nation's streets and highways, the president of the United States traveled at two speeds: fast and efficient to save time and minimize danger, and leisurely and slow to show himself to the crowds and wave to people as he drove by. On November 22, John Kennedy did not want anyone in Dallas to miss seeing him because his car was traveling too fast. Accordingly, the Secret Service had slowed the limousine to parade pace. This made the agents nervous. When the car was topless, as it was today, the agents preferred to ride

The motorcade drives through the streets of downtown Dallas, with crowds of spectators mere steps away from the presidential limousine. Curious bus passengers look down at John and Jackie Kennedy.

on the running boards — metal retractable shelves protruding from the sides of the car. They would also stand on the two steps at the rear of the limousine. Metal bars mounted to the body of the car provided handholds. Having agents stand on the Lincoln gave the president at least some protection. They could try to bat away any objects thrown at the president. Once, to their horror, someone tossed a bouquet of flowers into the car. It was harmless, but what if it had concealed a hand grenade? And their bodies could block gunfire. This was especially true of the two agents assigned to stand on the back steps behind the trunk. The presence of these agents would make it almost impossible for a sniper to shoot the president from behind. Had a Secret Service man happened to be standing on the right rear step when John Kennedy rode through Dealey Plaza, and had Lee Harvey Oswald chosen to shoot from behind the president, the agent's body would have obscured Oswald's sight line. The assassination attempt would have failed.

But President Kennedy did not like it when his bodyguards rode on the car because he thought it made him look less approachable to the people. On a number of occasions, he complained when agents did so. Today in Dallas, all the men in the security detail knew that they risked irritating the president if they rode on the outside of the car during the trip from Love Field, through downtown, through Dealey Plaza, and on to the Trade Mart. The Secret Service hated that open car. But the president and the people loved it.

The ride through Dallas was a triumph. There were no ugly incidents, and people cheered extra loud whenever the president drew near. Jackie put on her sunglasses. "The sun was so strong in our faces," she recalled. But her husband told her to take them off—the people wanted to see her face, he said.

Spectators waved and clapped. Many snapped photographs or took home movies, which did not record sound. The motorcade made two unscheduled stops. Children held up a homemade sign that asked the president to stop and greet them. When Kennedy spotted the sign, he shouted to his driver to step on the brakes. In the middle of a motorcade surrounded by thousands of onlookers, the gleaming Lincoln limousine halted. The Secret Service agents went on high alert, fearing that the president was about to get out of the car and stand up. JFK was famous for plunging into friendly crowds and leaving nervous bodyguards behind in his wake. If he did that now, thousands of excited people would rush forward to try to shake his hand. At Love Field, at least there was a fence. On this street, no barrier separated the president from the throng.

It was dangerous to stop a motorcade. In 1958, when Vice President Richard Nixon visited Venezuela, an anti-American mob intercepted his car, smashed the windows, almost tipped it over, and came close to murdering him and his wife. JFK had the good sense not to leave the car. The children were allowed to approach him. Then the limousine drove on. At a couple of points, Secret Service agent Clinton J. Hill hopped off the trail car and stepped onto the back of the presidential limousine, positioning himself behind Jackie. From that location he could leap off the car to intercept any pedestrian who rushed the Lincoln, and in that position his body would shield her and absorb any bullet fired at her from behind. After a short time, Agent

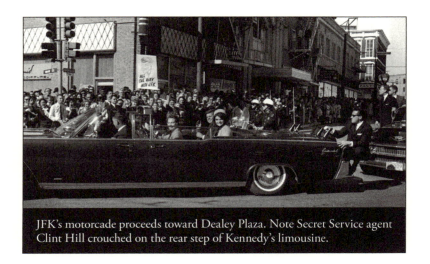

JFK's motorcade proceeds toward Dealey Plaza. Note Secret Service agent Clint Hill crouched on the rear step of Kennedy's limousine.

Hill stepped off the car and jumped back onto the running board of the trail car. Farther along the route, JFK spotted some Catholic nuns standing curbside. He ordered his driver to pull over for the sisters. A fellow Catholic, the president wanted to pay them his respects. Kennedy remained in the car and soon bade farewell to the delighted nuns.

• • •

Lee Harvey Oswald could see none of this. No one knows what was in his mind while, for the second time in his life, he prepared to kill a man. His sniper attack back in April on General Walker was an absurd failure. That night he was certain that he had his target fixed in the center of his telescopic sight, but his first shot had struck a piece of horizontal framing in the window that deflected the bullet's trajectory. Walker felt the whoosh of the bullet as it rocketed past his ear. Oswald must have wondered how he possibly could have missed. He had no time to fire a second shot. Lee hid his rifle and ran away into the night.

Alone, in the quiet of the sixth floor, did he think about the failed attempt on General Walker's life? Did he think of Marina and his two children one last time? Did he reconsider? Did he ask himself what on earth he was doing at this window with a rifle in his hands? The answers to these and other questions are lost to history: Oswald left behind no journal, diary, or manifesto, no last-minute letter of explanation or justification to his wife or to the country.

• • •

The president was running late. The handshaking at Love Field, plus the two stops for the clever children and the admiring nuns, had put him at least five or ten minutes behind schedule. Oswald waited by the window. Whenever his eyes searched Houston Street for the first signs of the motorcade, he was careful not to hold the rifle high in his hands. Someone on the ground might see him and warn the authorities.

Finally, the police motorcycles, their red lights flashing, and trailed by the lead car carrying the Dallas chief of police, reached the corner of Main and Houston and then turned right onto Houston. The Texas School Book Depository stood one block away. Oswald saw the motorcycles first. Then he saw the police chief's white car. Then he spotted what he had been waiting for—the big, gleaming midnight-blue limousine carrying the president of the United States. (Today, American presidents travel with two hardtop limousines—one a decoy, the other occupied by the president—to confuse potential assassins. In John Kennedy's era, there was only one.) And from the moment Oswald saw that car turn onto Houston Street, he knew with 100 percent certainty that one of its six occupants had to be John F. Kennedy. If Oswald fixed his gaze on the car, he must have noticed in the distance what appeared to be an unusually bright pinpoint of color toward the rear of the vehicle. It was Jacqueline Kennedy, her pink suit and pillbox hat glowing like a signal beacon. Indeed, he probably saw her first, before he spotted the president.

Inside the limousine, Nellie Connally was delighted with how well the day had gone. The motorcade had passed through the cheering crowds in downtown Dallas without incident. As the car drove closer to the Book Depository, she turned around to congratulate JFK: "You can't say that Dallas doesn't love you today, Mr. President." Kennedy looked at her and smiled.

• • •

From the moment Oswald saw the presidential limousine, he knew that the odds on his successfully assassinating President Kennedy had just tipped in his favor. Luck was with him that day. First, Kennedy had come to Dallas. Oswald would have never stalked him on a presidential trip to another city. But now the president had come to him. Who knew, five weeks earlier, before Kennedy's Dallas trip had even been planned, that Oswald would take a job at a building that turned out to be on the motorcade route? Even President Kennedy's itinerary proved lucky for Oswald. At any other time of day, the Book Depository employees working on the upper floors might have discovered Oswald hiding in his sniper's nest. But JFK would drive by during lunch hour, when the employees would vacate the upper floors and go down to eat or leave the building to watch as the president passed. By a little after noon, Oswald could expect to have the entire sixth floor to himself. But this advantage offered no guarantee of success.

Then he saw the limousine. It was a convertible. The bubble

top was off. This plastic top was not bulletproof anyway, but it might deflect a bullet. Only one fired at the perfect angle could penetrate it and harm the president. As fate would have it, Oswald would not have to worry about this. He could also see that no Secret Service agents stood on the back of the Lincoln. That meant Oswald would have a clear line of sight to John Kennedy. Nothing would block his view of the president.

But unbeknownst to Oswald, three other men who worked at the Book Depository were heading to one of the upper floors to get a bird's-eye view of the motorcade. They walked toward a window at the far southeast corner of the building, also knowing it would give them a great view straight up Houston Street as the president's car drove toward the Depository and then turned onto Elm right under their window. They approached the corner window. Would they discover Oswald with his rifle? No. They had stopped at the fifth floor. From their perch there, they had a commanding, unparalleled view of Dealey Plaza, better than anyone else waiting for President Kennedy that day. Except for the view enjoyed by the man who was waiting on the sixth floor — right above their heads.

• • •

The other cars following the president copied the turn onto Houston. Oswald could see a whole line of them now — the Secret Service car bearing eight agents plus longtime JFK aides Dave Powers and Ken O'Donnell, then the car carrying Vice President Johnson, then the other vehicles filled with the reporters, White House staff members, and others. All the passengers in Kennedy's car could see the Texas School Book Depository now, looming only one block ahead. And Oswald had a clear view of the president. He was now within range and getting closer with every passing second. Soon, Oswald could raise his rifle, place the crosshairs of his scope on Kennedy's forehead, and squeeze the trigger. One well-aimed shot through the head would be sure to kill him.

In Dealey Plaza, another man waited to get President Kennedy in his sights. He was Abraham Zapruder, a dress man-ufacturer whose office was nearby. He owned a portable color Bell & Howell 8mm movie camera, a popular compact recorder that served as the unofficial memory maker of the 1960s. Zapruder walked over to Dealey Plaza with one of his employees, a woman who had encouraged him to bring his camera and film

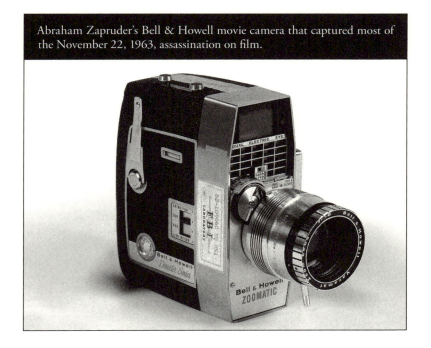

Abraham Zapruder's Bell & Howell movie camera that captured most of the November 22, 1963, assassination on film.

President Kennedy. Zapruder selected an optimal vantage point along Elm Street in the middle of the plaza, between the Book Depository and the triple underpass that led to the Stemmons Freeway. To get a better view above the heads of people gathering to see the president, Zapruder stood on top of a low concrete pedestal. He asked his employee to hold his legs and steady him once the president got close enough. It was the perfect spot. From here, Zapruder would enjoy a panoramic vista of the limousine from the time it turned onto Elm Street until it disappeared below the Stemmons Freeway underpass and out of range. When the police motorcycles leading the motorcade turned onto Elm Street and came within sight, Zapruder held down the RUN button of his camera and started shooting. To save film, he stopped after a few seconds to await President Kennedy.

• • •

Oswald waited too. He waited to get the president in his scope. If he shot now, as JFK drove toward him, he would have a very small margin of error. To hit a passenger in a vehicle moving toward him at so close a distance, Oswald would have to lower the barrel of his rifle in a dipping, continuous motion to keep his target sighted. His aim would have to be perfect. If he shot too low, he risked hitting the windshield or the metal horizontal crossbar above the middle of the car used to attach the top. If his aim was a little better, he might hit Governor John Connally, who sat in the jump seat in front of the president.

Only if his aim and timing were perfect would Oswald hit JFK. And he might get off only one shot. To fire a frontal shot, the assassin would have to step forward and poke his rifle through the open window. Even before he aimed and fired, he would be visible, in plain sight, to anyone in Chief Curry's car, in the presidential limousine, or in the Secret Service trail car. Kennedy's driver might take evasive action, swerving or accelerating to disrupt Oswald's aim. Agents might open fire on him, forcing him to duck for cover. The assassination would fail. And if Oswald got off a shot, the sound of gunfire would draw eyes to the upper floors of the Book Depository. If the first shot missed, he might not get to fire a second one. If the police or Secret Service were quick to pinpoint Oswald's location, he risked capture or death before he could even run down the stairs from the sixth floor to the first. No, the risk was too great. Oswald held his fire as he watched the president's limousine drive straight at him, until it reached the corner of Houston and Elm and slowed to make the hairpin left turn onto Elm.

Now the president was passing right below him. If Oswald leaned out of the window, aimed down, and fired as the president's car slowed to almost a stop to make the turn, he could hardly miss. But that would expose his position to the rest of the motorcade and to the people in the street. It must have been difficult for the impulsive Oswald to restrain himself.

He readied to take full advantage of his well-chosen sniper's nest. He allowed the president's car to make its turn undisturbed, followed by the Secret Service car. Now the shiny Lincoln entered Abraham Zapruder's field of vision, and the amateur cameraman started filming again.

Jackie Kennedy shifted her eyes away from the crowd and looked ahead a few blocks to the spot where Elm Street merged into the triple overpass. *Just a few more blocks,* she thought. Later she recalled, "[W]e saw this tunnel ahead, I thought it would be cool in the tunnel . . . the sun wouldn't get into your eyes."

As Oswald peered out the sixth-floor window and looked to his right, he was facing the president's back. The Marine Corps had trained him to shoot at targets at distances of two hundred, four hundred, and even six hundred yards—without the aid of a telescopic sight. Oswald positioned his body in a shooting stance—he could have been standing or kneeling—and thrust the barrel of his rifle through the window. He might have rested it on a cardboard box of schoolbooks to stabilize his aim. He pointed down and aimed for the back of John Kennedy's head—the only sure-kill shot.

Several eyewitnesses on the ground saw the barrel protruding from the window. One person thought it was a pipe. Another spotted a man at the window with a sneer on his face. The president was now in the crosshairs of Oswald's scope. This was it.

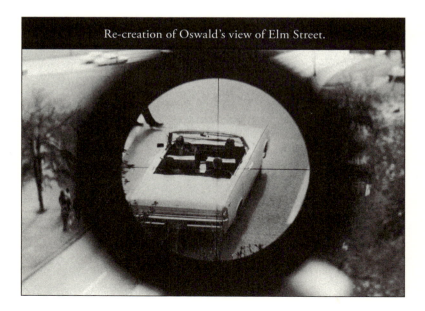

Re-creation of Oswald's view of Elm Street.

Oswald had not lost his nerve. He was really going to do it. He squeezed the trigger. *Never jerk the trigger back with a quick pull,* he learned in the Marine Corps. Squeeze the trigger slowly, apply gradual, increasing pressure, and when that pressure reached a few pounds, his trigger released the firing pin. It struck the rear of the bullet in the chamber, which instantaneously ignited the gunpowder in the brass cartridge case and spit a 6.5 mm conical, jacketed lead bullet traveling at seventeen or eighteen hundred feet per second at the president of the United States. John Kennedy was close—less than one hundred feet away. The Book Depository clock read 12:30 p.m. Abraham Zapruder's finger maintained constant pressure on his camera's RUN switch and he continued filming.

Through his telescopic sight, Oswald expected to see the evidence of his deed. But the president's body displayed no reaction to being hit by the bullet. He did not recoil from the impact, slump in his seat, or even twitch.

Oswald had missed!

Not only did he fail to shoot JFK, he was not even close. He did not hit Jackie, who was sitting a few feet to the president's left, nor did he hit Governor Connally, who was sitting in front of Kennedy. The shot was so off the mark that it had even failed to hit the car, which, at this close range, was a huge target in his scope.

• • •

In the car, John Kennedy heard the shot. At that moment, he stopped waving to the crowd and lowered his right arm. Jackie heard it too. She had been looking to her left at the people standing along the curb. At the sound of the gunfire, she spun her head to the right and looked to JFK's side of the car. "They were gunning the motorcycles," she remembered. "There were these little backfires. [Then] there was one noise like that. I thought it was a backfire."

Witnesses heard different things. To some people traveling in the motorcade, or to many bystanders along Elm Street, it sounded like a firecracker. *What kind of jerk would play a joke like that,* they wondered. To others, it sounded like a car or a motorcycle backfiring. To the pigeons atop the roof of the Depository, it was a sound of danger that caused them to flee to the skies. To others — some of the policemen, Secret Service agents, ex-military men, or hunters in Dealey Plaza that day — it sounded like something else. It was a rifle shot.

Abraham Zapruder heard it too. It caused him to jostle his camera involuntarily, almost imperceptibly. Through his viewfinder, he, like Oswald, observed no signs of distress to the president or the other passengers. He continued to film the car, keeping it in his sights as it moved slowly in front of him from left to right.

• • •

Lee Harvey Oswald had botched the first shot. The same man who had failed to assassinate General Walker had just failed in his attempt to assassinate the president of the United States. But how had he missed? Lee was too good a rifleman, and the limousine too close, for him to have missed it completely. Even if, in his excitement, he had rushed the first shot, he should have hit *someone* or *something* in the car. As much as chance had saved General Walker, it had just saved President Kennedy from the assassin's first bullet. At the moment Oswald had trained his scope on JFK, the presidential limousine had driven under an oak tree on the Book Depository side of Elm Street. For a few seconds, the tree's branches had acted as a semitransparent umbrella that stood between Oswald and Kennedy. Looking between the branches, Oswald could still see the president, so he had fired that first shot. But before it could find its target, the bullet had probably nicked a tree branch, which deflected its trajectory and probably stripped it of its outer metal jacket. Instead, the bullet struck a concrete curb beyond the limousine on the far side of Elm Street. The impact showered fragments into the air that hit a bystander, James Tague, in the face and made a small cut in his cheek.

Whatever the reason, the president had escaped Oswald's first shot unscathed. Anything might happen next. If Kennedy's driver hit the gas and accelerated the car from its present speed of twelve to fifteen miles per hour to just twenty-five or thirty miles per hour, he could spirit the president away from further danger. It might have been enough to just swerve the car violently from right to left. But the driver did not react. The leader of John Kennedy's Secret Service detail, sitting in the front passenger seat, could have ordered the driver to race out of Dealey Plaza. But he did not. The president himself—a decorated World War II navy veteran who had heard gunshots before—could have shouted orders to get himself out of there. But he did not.

What would Oswald do now? He could run away, just like he'd done that night at General Walker's house. If he stepped back from the window and withdrew his rifle, he could hide it between the boxes and return to work and pretend that nothing had happened. If no one on the ground had seen him, and if witnesses convinced themselves that the sound had been nothing more than a firecracker or engine backfire, then police might not even investigate the Book Depository. He might escape. Lee Harvey Oswald could go home that night and scold himself for yet another failed attempt to become part of history.

But Oswald did not have a faint heart in Dallas that afternoon. He did not release his grip on the rifle. At the limousine's present speed and direction, the president would be within range for the next ten to twelve seconds. The clock had started ticking with Oswald's first shot. Now he prepared to fire a second one.

With his right hand, he grasped the bolt, raised it, pulled it back, and ejected the empty brass cartridge casing, which popped into the air and made a hollow ping when it landed on the wood floor. The ejection of the cartridge caused a spring in the clip to push another round into position in front of the bolt. Oswald slammed the bolt forward, chambered the round, and turned the bolt handle down. He had practiced this movement countless times and had distilled it into one quick, fluid motion.

It was easy to locate the president in his scope. The car was traveling at a slow speed in almost a straight line down Elm Street away from the sixth-floor window. Thus Oswald did not have to swing his rifle from left to right to track a target moving horizontally. The car's speed and direction created for Oswald the advantage of an optical illusion in which the car seemed almost a stationary object that was slowly getting smaller. All he needed to do was make a small vertical adjustment. He raised the barrel of his rifle a few degrees. For the second time, he took aim at the back of John Kennedy's head. Almost 2.7

seconds had elapsed since Oswald had fired the first shot. No one in the presidential entourage had reacted to it yet. Abraham Zapruder continued to film the motorcade. For a few moments, Kennedy disappeared from Zapruder's viewfinder — a large Stemmons Freeway roadside sign temporarily blocked his view of the limousine and President Kennedy. For the second time, Oswald squeezed the trigger. 3 seconds. The president was 190 feet away. 3.4 seconds. The rifle fired.

He missed the head again!

But this time his marksmanship proved better. This second bullet had come within about ten inches of striking JFK's head. But Oswald's aim had been slightly off target. Instead, the bullet struck the president in the upper back, to the right of his spine, and bored a tunnel through his body at a downward angle — because Oswald was shooting from high above the car — and it exited through his lower throat. John Kennedy's tissue absorbed some of the bullet's energy, causing it to leave his body at a slower speed than it had entered it — fifteen to sixteen hundred feet per second. Then the bullet, still deadly, began to tumble in mid-air and struck Governor Connally in the back, exited his chest at nine hundred feet per second, hit his wrist, and then, slowed to four hundred feet per second, lodged in his thigh. Lee Oswald's bullet had traveled through the bodies of two men and had inflicted serious wounds to both. These multiple impacts had deformed the bullet's shape, but it was still in one piece. Although they had just been shot, President Kennedy and Governor Connally were still alive and conscious . . . and might survive.

If the president had heard this shot, his auditory senses did not register it until after he felt the impact of the bullet. And if he had heard it, he would have known that it was a rifle and that he was in the process of being assassinated. No one could doubt the sound of gunfire now. Secret Service agents standing on the running board of the trail car turned their heads and looked over their right shoulders at the Book Depository. Both shots sounded as though they had come from behind them. A moment after the second shot, a news photographer snapped a picture of the front of Kennedy's limousine and of the Secret Service trail car, freezing the agents in position with their heads turned back to the Depository.

The photograph shows something else. The gunshot propelled President Kennedy's elbows and forearms up, parallel to the ground, and pushed his clenched fists, thumbs down, toward his throat. He could not move his arms from this position — they were locked in place by nerve damage. In the photo, a white-gloved hand — Jackie Kennedy's — touches the president's left forearm.

Abraham Zapruder did not capture on film the moment the president was shot. When Kennedy disappeared behind the Stemmons Freeway sign, he was uninjured. When he emerged from behind the sign, he had already raised his arms. If not for the obscuring sign, Zapruder would have captured the exact moment Oswald's second bullet wounded the president. Zapruder kept filming.

Jackie Kennedy knew something was wrong. Wounded, Governor Connally, an experienced hunter, already knew. He shouted, "No, no, no!" and "They're going to kill us all!" A Secret Service agent riding in the trail car saw the bullet hit the president and tear a hole in the back of his suit coat. Jackie rotated her body toward her husband. She held his left forearm in her hands. Puzzled, she looked at Governor Connally, who was twisting strangely in his seat. Then she faced her husband again. The startled, wide-eyed expression on his face frightened her. She leaned in closer. Their eyes were just inches apart. Then she said: "What's wrong, Jack?" He did not answer. He could not speak.

• • •

Lee Harvey Oswald operated the bolt of his rifle and ejected a second brass cartridge onto the floor. He chambered a third round. He elevated the barrel a few degrees. Oswald took his time. This shot might be his last. He still had a fourth and final bullet in the clip. But he would probably not have the opportunity to fire it before Kennedy's car drove out of range, especially if it sped up to interfere with his aim. More time elapsed since the first shot. 6 seconds now.

• • •

Secret Service agent Clint Hill, riding the left-rear running board of the trail car, knew what was wrong. He leaped off the car and sprinted for the presidential limousine. Fellow agents rooted for him to close the distance before the sniper could fire a third shot. Hill ran as fast as he could. The thirty-one-year-old agent had been with Mrs. Kennedy from the beginning and had protected her on trips all over the world. He had to help her now. She was sitting so close to the president that another rifle shot might blow her head off. If only Hill could get between the Kennedys and the sniper before he fired another shot. Hill, who was not wearing a bulletproof vest, could block the bullet with his own body and save the president. It was a sacrifice that he would be happy to make. He was an excellent athlete and closed on the president's car fast. Just a few more yards, and he could grab for the big handle on the trunk and yank himself up on the rear foothold. If he could do that he would be a human shield — the assassin would have to shoot through him to get the president. Only Jackie's agent could save John Kennedy now — the president's own Secret Service agent had not yet left the trail car. 7 seconds.

Oswald's second shot was not necessarily fatal. It had not struck Kennedy's head, spine, or heart. His other vital organs — lungs, liver, kidneys, spleen — were undamaged. The chief danger to the president was shock and loss of blood. But it was a survivable wound. Many soldiers in World War II and the Korean War had survived worse injuries. If the driver gunned the engine and increased the car's speed to eighty miles per hour, the president could be in the emergency room of nearby Parkland Hospital in less than ten minutes.

8 seconds. Oswald began to squeeze the trigger. The Newman family, two young parents and their two small children, were standing just a few feet away from the president. Abraham Zapruder kept filming. Nellie Connally held her husband in her arms. As he lost consciousness, he believed that he was dying. Bystander Mary Moorman raised her Polaroid camera and prepared to click the shutter. Clint Hill knew he would make it in just a couple more steps. The president remained upright in the backseat. He had not spoken a word. The driver did not race away to escape the gunfire. Instead, the limousine

seemed to slow down. Jackie Kennedy gazed into her husband's uncomprehending eyes. They had been married ten years that fall.

8.4 seconds. The rifle fired.

This time Oswald did not miss.

The third bullet sliced through John Kennedy's thatch of thick reddish-brown hair. It cut a neat hole through his scalp and perforated his skull. The velocity, the pressure, and the physics of death did the rest. The right rear side of the president's skull blew out—exploded, really—tearing open his scalp, and spewing skull fragments, blood, and brains several feet into the air where it hung for a few seconds, suspended in a pink cloud. It splattered the motorcycle windshield and face of a police officer

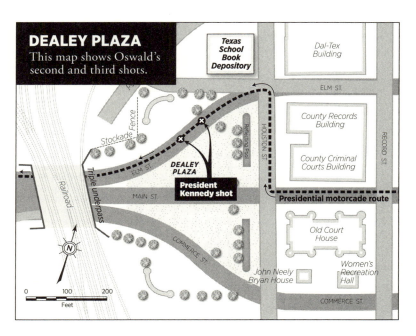

DEALEY PLAZA
This map shows Oswald's second and third shots.

Texas School Book Depository

Dal-Tex Building

ELM ST.

Stockade Fence

Reflecting Pool

County Records Building

HOUSTON ST.

RECORD ST.

County Criminal Courts Building

ELM ST.

DEALEY PLAZA

President Kennedy shot

Presidential motorcade route

Railroad

Triple underpass

MAIN ST.

Old Court House

COMMERCE ST.

N

Women's Recreation Hall

John Neely Bryan House

0   100   200
Feet

COMMERCE ST.

riding close to the left side of the car.

This shot, the president of the United States never heard. He lost consciousness the moment the bullet hit him. As his limp body began to tip toward his wife, her mouth opened wide in shock. "Oh, no!" she exclaimed. She was so close to her husband when he was wounded for the second time that her hair, face, gloves, and pink suit were all stained with gore. "I could see a piece of his skull coming off," she said. "It was flesh-colored, not white . . . I can see this . . . piece detaching itself from his head. Then he slumped in my lap; his blood and brains were in my lap." The scene traumatized Jackie for the rest of her life.

• • •

Oswald, his eye glued to his rifle scope, must have seen the spray of red mist. Then he operated the bolt, ejected the third cartridge case, and chambered the fourth round. He was ready to shoot again. He paused, then stepped away from the window. His work, he decided, was done. Now it was time to escape.

• • •

Jackie Kennedy panicked. She glimpsed that something had fallen on the dark blue, mirrored finish of the limousine trunk. It was a piece of her husband's skull. She rose from the backseat, turned around, kneeled on the seat, and reached onto the trunk. She was fully exposed to the assassin now. If Oswald had lingered in the window and desired to fire a fourth shot, he could have used his last bullet to kill Jackie. Still kneeling on the backseat, she stretched her body toward the skull fragment. The president, she might have convinced herself, would need that when the doctors fixed him at the hospital.

Taken moments after Oswald fired his third shot and retreated from the window, this photograph shows two of the three Book Depository employees who watched the motorcade from the fifth-floor windows. They heard the shots fired from the floor above them and the sound of cartridge cases hitting the wood floor above their heads.

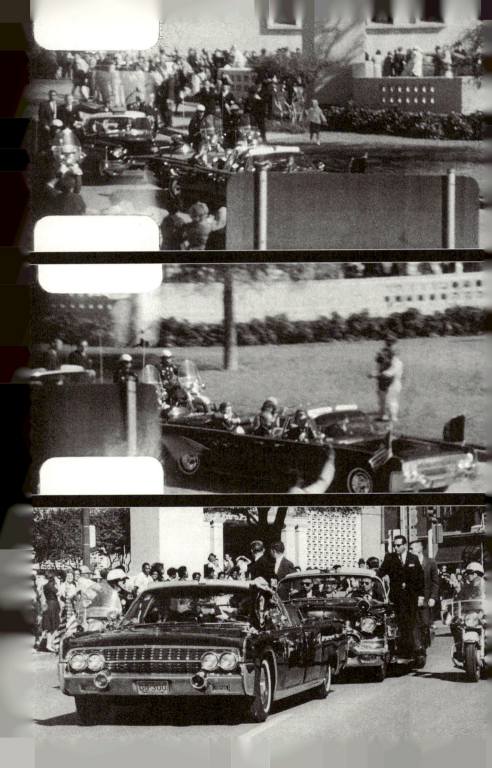

Zapruder filmed the president waving, just before he disappeared behind a road sign. (The frames from Zapruder's film can be identified by the sprocket holes on the left side of his pictures.)

As the president emerges from behind the sign, we see that he's already been hit by the bullet that entered his back. His arms are raised from the bullet wound. Jackie, knowing something is wrong, looks at her husband.

News reporter James Altgens photographed the limousine just after the president had been shot and had raised his arms. Note Jackie's white-gloved hand touching his left arm. Secret Service agents look back at the Book Depository. Agent Clint Hill (in sunglasses) looks at Jackie.

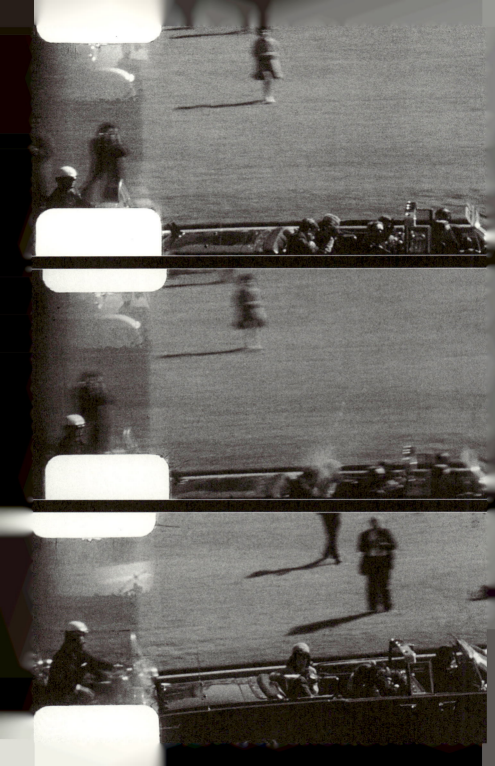

In this Zapruder frame, Jackie leans in close to JFK to find out what is wrong. Their faces are inches apart.

The moment of impact of the deadly bullet.

The president slumps over as Jackie looks on. She gasps in horror and cries out, "Oh, no!"

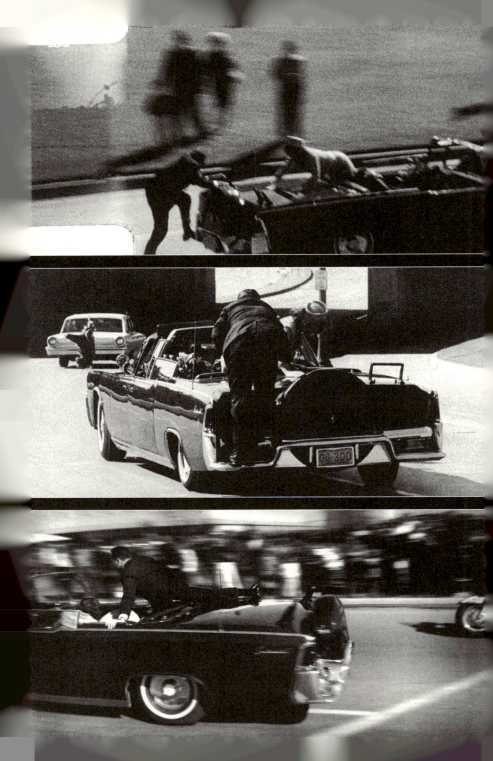

Agent Clint Hill jumps on the back of the moving limousine as Jackie Kennedy begins to climb out of the rear seat of the car.

Agent Hill pushes Jackie back into the rear seat.

Agent Hill shields the Kennedys with his body as the limousine speeds away from Dealey Plaza to Parkland Hospital.

Clint Hill could not believe what he was seeing. If the car accelerated now, Jackie might be thrown onto the trunk, fall to the pavement, and get run over by the Secret Service car. He lunged forward and caught one of the handles mounted on the back of the limousine. He'd made it! But at that moment, the car lurched forward and Hill lost his footing. Unless he released his grip, in another second the car would drag him down to the pavement. But he would not leave Mrs. Kennedy. He mustered all the strength he had and pulled hard against the handle, yanked his body up, and caught a tenuous foothold on the step. Then he launched his body across the trunk, gathered Jackie in his arms and pushed her back into the car. He used his body to cover her and the president. Later, Jackie had no memory of this terrifying scene. Clint Hill never forgot it: the president was lying face up in her lap, and she shouted: "My God, they have shot his head off!"

Hill looked at JFK, appalled at what he saw: "The right rear portion of his head was missing." As the car sped away, other agents saw Hill pound his fist on the trunk and shake his head in despair. Then he signaled them with a thumbs-down. The president's car accelerated and, along with the trailing Secret Service car, reached the shadows of the triple underpass and disappeared from the view of the dumbfounded witnesses in Dealey Plaza and the rest of the motorcade.

In Vice President Johnson's car, Secret Service agent Rufus Youngblood yelled, "Get down!" and pushed LBJ to the floor and covered him with his body to protect him from gunfire. The car raced after the others. Inside, Lyndon Johnson had no idea whether President Kennedy was dead or alive.

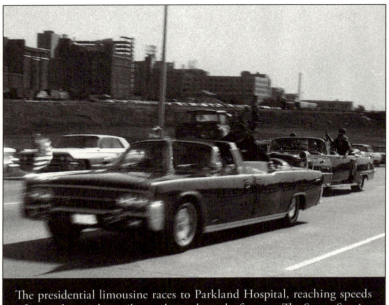

The presidential limousine races to Parkland Hospital, reaching speeds of more than eighty miles per hour along the freeway. The Secret Service trail car follows.

• • •

Lee Oswald abandoned his three spent brass cartridges where they fell, and, still holding his rifle, ran the diagonal length of the sixth floor, heading for the back stairs. He shoved the weapon into a narrow space between two stacks of boxes. Now, as he raced down the stairs, he was in possession of no evidence that, if he were searched, would link him to the shooting. Oswald descended the floors — fifth, fourth, third — and encountered no one coming up. When he reached the second floor, he must have heard someone below him coming up the stairs, so he ducked into the lunchroom. A Dallas policeman, the first one to enter the Depository after the shooting, found the building manager, Roy Truly. Together, they hurried up the stairs. When the policeman reached the second floor, he spotted

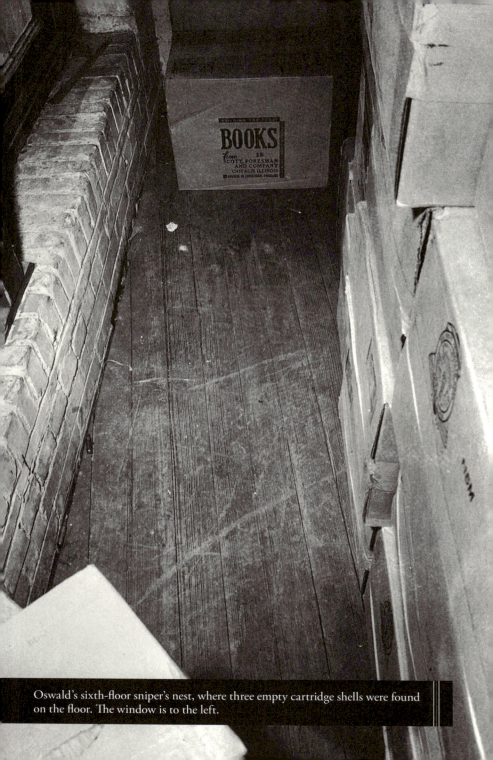

Oswald's sixth-floor sniper's nest, where three empty cartridge shells were found on the floor. The window is to the left.

Oswald through a window in the lunchroom door, ordered him to stop, and asked the manager if Oswald worked there. When Truly answered yes, the policeman let Oswald go and continued racing to the roof.

Oswald was lucky. It was a spectacular error of logic for the officer to assume that no one employed at the Depository could have shot the president. Oswald descended to the first floor and walked out the front door onto Elm Street. At that moment, a man grabbed Oswald — the assassin feared that the man was a Secret Service agent — but he only asked Oswald where he could find the nearest telephone. It was just a reporter. The helpful assassin gave him directions. Then, as policemen and citizens converged at the front door of the Texas School Book Depository, and as Dealey Plaza devolved into a chaos of sirens, police radios, shouting, and people running in every direction — Lee Harvey Oswald strolled away from the scene of his crime. He had shot the president, and he had, at least for now, escaped.

• • •

In the press car, a famous White House reporter, Merriman Smith, grabbed the radio-telephone mounted in the front seat. Three minutes after Oswald's first shot, Smith communicated a brief message to his employer, United Press International, a news service that distributed reports to media outlets all over the world. At 12:34 p.m. (CST), a UPI bulletin flashed the news across the country: "THREE SHOTS WERE FIRED TODAY AT PRESIDENT KENNEDY'S MOTORCADE IN DOWN-TOWN DALLAS." Ten minutes after the shooting, at 12:40 p.m.

(CST), at the New York headquarters of CBS News, the television network interrupted its regular programming and displayed its company logo on television screens across the nation tuned to the CBS network. The voice of Walter Cronkite, one of the most important journalists on television, spoke in an urgent, clipped tone: "Here is a bulletin from CBS News. In Dallas, Texas, three shots were fired at President Kennedy's motorcade in downtown Dallas. The first reports say that President Kennedy has been seriously wounded by this shooting."

The network did not have the technology to interrupt scheduled, pretaped programming and get Cronkite's face on the air immediately. At first, CBS could only broadcast his voice. Seconds after Cronkite announced the news, another printed bulletin was thrust into his hands. Listeners could hear him shuffling papers as he spoke: "More details just arrived. These details about the same as previously. President Kennedy shot today just as his motorcade left downtown Dallas. Mrs. Kennedy jumped up and grabbed Mr. Kennedy. She called, 'Oh, no!' The motorcade sped on. United Press says that the wounds for President Kennedy perhaps could be fatal."

Within a few minutes, the network was able to broadcast both image and sound, and Cronkite appeared on camera and continued to read news bulletins. It was the beginning of four unprecedented days of television coverage. Within one hour of the shooting, more than three quarters of the American people knew what had happened.

• • •

While Lee Oswald walked down Elm Street, President Kennedy's car raced to Parkland Hospital. Dallas police officers radioed ahead to advise the emergency room staff to stand by for a severe gunshot wound. On the hands of a clock, it was a brief ride. In the minds of the five unwounded passengers, it seemed to go on forever. The two Secret Service agents in the front seat could do nothing to help the president but get him to Parkland as fast as possible, reaching speeds of more than eighty miles per hour. In the jump seats behind the agents, Nellie Connally tended to her stricken husband. His wounds were painful, he was losing blood, and he lapsed in and out of consciousness. As Nellie held him in her arms, she promised him that everything would be all right.

Behind the Connallys, the backseat was a tangle of intertwined arms and legs and bodies. After Clint Hill had saved Jackie from falling off the trunk and pushed her back inside the car, she grabbed the president and held him close. Hill got on top of Jackie and the president to shield them from further gunfire. In his awkward spread-eagle position over JFK and Jackie, it was hard to hang on as the car reached top speed. The wind blew the sunglasses off Hill's face. Jackie cried out, "They've shot his head off! I have his brains in my hands." Then she spoke to her husband: "Jack, Jack, can you hear me? I love you, Jack." He could not hear her. "Jack, Jack, what have they done to you?" she implored. He did not answer.

Under Hill's human shield, the Kennedys rode to Parkland in contorted, sideways positions, lying partly on the backseat and partly on the floor. Blood pooled in the footwells of the floor. Jackie tried to close the gaping wound with her hands. "I tried to hold the top of his head down, maybe I could keep it in . . . but I knew he was dead." She remembered the puzzled, astonished look that Oswald's bullet had frozen on the president's face: "His head was so beautiful," she said.

• • •

Less than ten minutes after the third shot, the presidential limousine careened into the emergency room driveway at Parkland Hospital, followed by the Secret Service trail car and the vice president's vehicle. Agents leaped out with guns drawn. One agent brandished an automatic rifle. At the entrance, no medical carts awaited the stricken president. Some Secret Service agents ran inside and yelled for a cart. Hospital staffers rolled two to the car. They lifted the broken body of Governor Connally from his seat, and his wife exited the vehicle. The president's bodyguards wanted to snatch him from the backseat as quickly as they could and rush him inside. Time, they believed, was of the essence. Once Clint Hill got out of the car, the other agents got a clear view of the backseat for the first time. Other cars from the motorcade arrived at Parkland. Dave Powers, a longtime top political aide to JFK, ran up to the limousine, looked inside, and gasped: "Oh, my God, Mr. President!"

Agents bent over Kennedy to lift him out of the car. Jackie would not let him go. She had wrapped her arms tight around him and cradled his head in her lap. She curled over him in a protective embrace. She ignored the agents' request. Please, they told her, they needed to get the president inside so the doctors could treat him. Clint Hill, the agent she trusted most, beseeched her to release her husband.

"Please, Mrs. Kennedy," he said.

She would not budge.

"Please," Hill begged, "we must get the president to a doctor."

Jackie said no. "I'm not going to let him go . . . you know he's dead. Let me alone."

Hill's intuition and close relationship with Jackie told him why she was covering her husband's head with her arms and her body. She did not want anyone to see him that way. Hill showed her he understood. He removed his suit coat. "Hill threw his coat over Jack's head," she remembered, "and I held his head to throw the coat over it." Now no one would see the president's horrible wound, or his eyes fixed wide open in a stare.

Jackie released her hold and Secret Service men lifted John Kennedy's unconscious body from the backseat. They brought him inside the hospital at 12:38 p.m. (CST). It was eight minutes since he had been shot.

• • •

Lee Harvey Oswald was on the run. But he did not have much of an escape plan. If he had owned a car, he could have driven out of the city, and as far away from Dallas as he could get, possibly fleeing the country to Mexico. But he did not have a car; he did not even know how to drive. Lee Harvey Oswald was no John Wilkes Booth, Abraham Lincoln's assassin. Booth had a fast horse standing by at Ford's Theatre and the names and locations of sympathizers who might help him during his escape south from Washington. Oswald had no one. He walked seven blocks on Elm Street, then, at 12:40 p.m. (CST), he flagged down a passing city bus that was headed in the direction he wanted to go. Although Oswald was not standing at a scheduled bus stop, the driver opened the door and let him board anyway.

Its route would take Oswald past the Book Depository, back to the scene of his crime. He might have enjoyed witnessing the chaos he had created. Before the bus could get near the Depository, heavy traffic slowed its pace to almost a standstill.

It was absurd. The man who had just shot the president was stuck in traffic, trying to flee on a public bus. Realizing the ridiculousness of his position, Oswald stood up, walked to the front of the bus, and asked the driver to let him off. Within a few minutes, at about 12:47 p.m. (CST), he caught a taxi to his rooming house. When he arrived, the housekeeper was watching news of the assassination on television. She told Oswald that Kennedy had been shot. He said nothing. He hurried to his room, changed jackets, and picked up his revolver and some ammunition. Then, after a couple of minutes, he left at 1:03 p.m. (CST) without saying a word. No one knows what Oswald planned to do next. Perhaps he hoped to get to the bus station and buy a ticket to Mexico—he still had enough money on him for that, although not for anything more. If he hoped to escape capture, he needed to flee Dallas.

Soon, a roll call of employees at the Book Depository would reveal that only one man could not be accounted for—Lee Harvey Oswald.

• • •

At Parkland Hospital, Secret Service agents and hospital staffers rushed John Kennedy into Trauma Room 1. They lifted him from the cart and laid him on his back upon the examination table. Nurses cut away his clothing. Doctors looked for his vital signs. He had no blood pressure. He was not breathing. His

Oswald's rooming house, where he stopped to change clothes and pick up his revolver and ammunition.

heartbeat was sporadic and weak. The pupils of his eyes were dilated and fixed. The doctors inserted tubes into his veins. They cut a tracheotomy in his throat to improve his breathing. From throughout Parkland Hospital, doctors rushed to the emergency room. Some thought they could help. Others were unneeded voyeurs who wanted only to lay eyes upon the president so that one day they could say that they had been there.

• • •

While doctors worked on the president, some of the Secret Service agents worked on the car. To prevent curiosity seekers from peering into the backseat, or news reporters from snapping photographs of the blood and gore, agents mounted a top—a hardtop and not the clear plastic bubble top—to the convertible. Then they got steel buckets filled with water and towels and began to wash the backseat and the floor.

It was a stupid thing to do. The car was a crime scene and full of evidence. Everything in it, including possible bullet fragments,

At Parkland Hospital, Secret Service agents attached a hardtop to the limousine and tried to wash away the president's blood.

should have been left as is and preserved for the investigation that was sure to follow the assassination. It was as though they believed, through some faulty logic, that if they could just wipe away the evidence of the crime, they could turn back the clock and pretend that it had never happened. Try as they might, the agents could not wash away all the blood. It was like a scene from *Macbeth*, Shakespeare's play of murder and revenge, when "all great Neptune's ocean" would not "wash this blood clean from my hand." Jackie recalled what else lay in the car: "Every time we got off the plane that day, three times they gave me the yellow roses of Texas. But in Dallas they gave me red roses. I thought, how funny, red roses — so the seat was full of blood and red roses."

• • •

Jackie Kennedy approached the trauma room and tried to enter. "I'm not going to leave him. I'm not going to leave him," she told Dave Powers. A burly nurse tried to block her way. It was against hospital policy for family members to enter the room. Jackie told her she was going in and pushed the nurse. The nurse pushed back. "I want to be with him when he dies," Jackie insisted.

A navy admiral on the president's staff rushed to her aid. "It is her right," he commanded. "It is her prerogative." The nurse shrank away. Jackie walked into the room where desperate surgeons worked to save her husband's life.

The appearance of the president's wife, a haunting pale figure in the bright pink suit, shocked the doctors. One of them suggested that she might want to leave and wait outside. "But . . . it's my husband," she said. "His blood, his brains are all over me." It streaked her face, saturated her white gloves, and stained her suit and stockings. She nudged one of the doctors, and without speaking she held out her cupped hands. She was holding a part of the president's brain. Dazed, in shock, perhaps she thought they would need it. Maybe they could put it back inside his head. She handed it to the doctor. If John Kennedy had been any other patient, the doctors would have already pronounced him dead, perhaps even dead on arrival at Parkland Hospital. But this was the president of the United States — they had to try everything. As a last resort, one of the surgeons began to massage the president's heart, hoping to stimulate a rhythmic beat. It was too late. He was dead.

"I am sorry, Mrs. Kennedy," said one of the doctors, "your husband has sustained a mortal wound."

"I know," she whispered.

The doctors recorded the time of death as 1:00 p.m. (CST). One by one, members of the medical team left the trauma room. A nurse handed two paper bags to one of the Secret Service agents. They contained John Kennedy's suit coat, pants, shirt, tie, and other garments. The agent was also given Clint Hill's bloodstained suit coat. As the room emptied, Jackie Kennedy approached the table on which her husband lay dead. She pressed her cheek against his still warm face. She kissed his body. Then she removed her wedding ring and slipped it onto one of his fingers.

• • •

Within minutes, news of Kennedy's death flashed across America. At 1:38 p.m. (CST), a visibly shaken Walter Cronkite appeared on CBS television and made this announcement: "From Dallas, Texas, the flash, apparently official: President

Walter Cronkite of CBS News announces President Kennedy's death to the nation.

Kennedy died at one p.m., central standard time, two o'clock, eastern standard time—some thirty-eight minutes ago."

Across the nation, people at home that afternoon sat in their living rooms, riveted by television and radio alerts. Others gathered in quiet groups around office televisions and radios. Millions of people working that day were out to lunch when Kennedy was shot, and they heard the news when restaurants tuned their TVs and radios to news broadcasts. On the streets, many people gathered in front of appliance stores and watched the silent televisions on display behind plate-glass windows. Drivers stopped in traffic and got out of their cars to talk to other drivers. When newspapers started publishing special editions that afternoon, frantic customers snapped up the copies as soon as they were delivered to newsstands, drugstores, and other

KENNEDY EXT
PRESIDENT
Shot by Assa
Highlights of Kennedy's Career

On the evening of November 22, riders on a New York commuter train read newspaper accounts of the assassination on their way home from work.

New Yorkers gather at an electronics store to watch news broadcasts about the assassination.

In Dallas — and all across America — crowds thronged newsstands on the afternoon of November 22. Many vendors sold all their newspapers within minutes.

outlets. In Chicago, one man ripped an outdoor, red metal news box for the *Chicago American* right out of the ground and drove off with a stolen stack of papers announcing the assassination.

• • •

In Dallas, it was time to send for a casket. The Secret Service ordered one from a local funeral home. While it was on its way, hospital staffers washed the president's body and wrapped his head in towels and sheets of plastic so his blood would not stain the silk lining of the coffin. Then they wrapped the entire body. Mrs. Kennedy did not watch this. When the coffin arrived, funeral home workers wheeled it into the emergency room.

They lifted Kennedy's corpse from the table and laid it in the coffin. Then they closed the lid. The president was ready to go home to Washington.

As Secret Service agents began to roll the coffin through the emergency room to the white hearse waiting outside, a local Dallas official blocked their way. He told them that they could not remove the body. This was a murder, and the law was clear. An autopsy would have to be performed here in Texas before the agents could transport the corpse to Air Force One at Love Field and fly it to Washington. The agents and members of the president's personal staff were outraged. How dare this petty official try to stop them from taking the president home?

The arrival of other Texas officials did not break the logjam. The dispute almost broke out into a fistfight until, at 2:08 p.m. (CST), the Secret Service agents rolled the heavy coffin forward, right past the state officials, out the door, and into the hearse. John Kennedy's loyalists had no way of knowing that they had made a serious mistake. Their interference, and the resulting failure to conduct an autopsy in Dallas a few hours after the murder, would come to haunt the history of John Kennedy's assassination for the next fifty years. The intense display of emotions by Kennedy's grieving staff and Secret Service detail at Parkland Hospital, although understandable, served the nation poorly, and would, in time, and for decades to come, create widespread mistrust about the facts of the assassination, and encourage many wild theories about the murder.

• • •

After Lee Oswald left his boardinghouse, he set out on foot. By coincidence, a Dallas policeman driving his car through the neighborhood spotted Oswald walking on the sidewalk. The police officer, J. D. Tippit, knew that the president had been shot and had heard over his car radio a physical description of the suspect obtained from witnesses who had seen the man in the Book Depository window. Oswald matched it in a general way, so Tippit decided to pull over to the curb and have a word with him. The thirty-nine-year-old policeman stopped the car and called out to Oswald through the open passenger-side window. Oswald approached, leaned on the top edge of the passenger door, and conversed with Tippit. Then the officer got out of the car and started to walk around the front hood toward Oswald.

A moment later, at 1:15 p.m. (CST), Oswald pulled his revolver from his jacket pocket, aimed it at the policeman's chest, and opened fire. He had taken Tippit by surprise and shot him three times before the policeman could even draw his own pistol. Tippit collapsed to the ground. Oswald paused and then walked over to the wounded policeman. He was still alive. Then Oswald

Scene of the murder of Dallas police officer J. D. Tippit.

pointed his pistol at the helpless officer, shot him in the head, and killed him. Several witnesses either saw Oswald shoot Tippit, or flee the scene. One heard him mutter "poor dumb cop" or "poor damn cop." Some of them followed him, and then, from a safe distance, began chasing him. Less than two hours after the assassination, but without knowing that they were in pursuit of the president's killer, a small posse of citizens chased Oswald through the streets of Dallas. Soon, they lost track of him.

• • •

As soon as John Kennedy was pronounced dead, the Secret Service rushed Lyndon Johnson out of Parkland Hospital and drove him to Love Field. Johnson waited aboard Air Force One for the hearse carrying Kennedy's body to arrive at the airport. He was already aboard the plane before the Kennedy entourage left the hospital at 2:08 p.m. (CST). Johnson's advisers urged that he fly back to Washington right away and leave Mrs. Kennedy behind to catch Air Force Two, the vice presidential jet, later in the day. In one of his first acts as chief executive, he decided that he would not fly back to Washington at once and abandon Mrs. Kennedy in Dallas. Because she refused to leave without her husband's corpse, and because Johnson refused to leave without her, he ordered Air Force One to wait. All of them would fly back together. Johnson also decided that he would take the oath of office on the ground in Dallas before the plane took off.

The hearse drove onto the field. The modest motorcade from the hospital to the airport was not as grand as the one that had left Love Field for downtown Dallas just two hours ago. Jackie refused to be separated from the coffin, so she and Clint Hill sat next to it in the hearse. At the airport, Kennedy's aides

President Kennedy's casket is carried aboard Air Force One by Secret Service agents and members of his staff.

and Secret Service agents carried the heavy coffin up the stairs of an airline ramp and onto the plane. They could barely lift it — it weighed eight hundred pounds, not counting the added weight of the president's body. Then it would not fit through the airplane door — it was too wide. To make the coffin narrower, they broke the handles off its sides so they could push it onto the plane. They secured it in a small cabin near the back, where some seats had been removed to accommodate it. Again, Jackie sat beside her husband.

Although the coffin was now on board, Lyndon Johnson did not want Air Force One to depart Dallas until he took the oath of office and was sworn in as the thirty-sixth president of the United States. Johnson, a Texan, had summoned an old friend, a local federal district court judge named Sarah T. Hughes, to rush over to Love Field to swear him in.

In fact, Johnson did not need to take the oath in order to assume the office — by authority of the United States Constitution he had already become president upon the death of his predecessor. The swearing in was a formality to confirm what had already happened. But Lyndon Johnson wanted to take the oath at once as a symbol of the continuity of the American government. A president might die, but democracy would live. And he wanted the ceremony photographed to transmit that symbol around the world. A White House photographer, Captain Cecil Stoughton, was aboard the plane. He loaded two cameras with film and planned in his head where he and the new president should stand in the cramped cabin to create the most solemn and impressive photograph. The image would convey that Johnson was now in charge of the government.

By tradition, when a president took the oath of office he stood alone, raised his right hand, and repeated the words of the oath spoken to him by the chief justice of the Supreme Court of the United States. On November 22, Lyndon Johnson had something else in mind. He wanted two people standing by his side. One was his wife, Lady Bird. The other was Jackie Kennedy. It was a bold and, in the opinion of some of President Kennedy's staffers, an outrageous and offensive request. How could a woman widowed just hours ago, under the most horrible of circumstances, be expected to pose for pictures? Johnson realized that his request demanded sensitivity, delicacy, and tact. Before he became vice president, when he was a United States senator and held the powerful post of majority leader, he was renowned for his legendary skill at persuading other people to do what he asked. But it was one thing to strong-arm a fellow politician in a backroom deal over a piece of legislation in Congress, and quite another to handle the bereaved first lady of the United States, who was still in a state of shock after seeing her husband murdered in front of her eyes. LBJ sensed he could not delegate this request to others. He would have to appeal to Jackie himself.

Lyndon and Lady Bird Johnson went to Jacqueline Kennedy's private compartment to offer their condolences. "Dear God, it's come to this," said Lady Bird. Jackie said that she was grateful that her husband did not die alone: "Oh, what if I had not been there. Oh, I am so glad I was there." Lady Bird asked her if she would like to change into fresh clothes.

"No," the new widow replied, "I want them to see what they have done to Jack."

Then LBJ broached the awkward subject. "Well—about the swearing in," he said. Jackie indicated that she understood: "Oh, yes, I know, I know. What's going to happen?" Johnson explained that he had summoned a federal judge to administer the presidential oath aboard Air Force One before the plane flew back to Washington. LBJ wanted her standing by his side. It was for history. Believing that she had agreed, Johnson left her alone to compose herself before Judge Hughes arrived.

More than one person suggested to Jackie that she change clothes. Her suit, white gloves, and stockings were caked with dried blood. No, she insisted, she would not change. "I want them to see what they've done," she repeated more than once.

To prepare for the swearing-in ceremony, she retired to her small bathroom. There, she said, "I saw myself in the mirror; my whole face was spattered with blood and hair . . . I wiped it off with Kleenex . . . then one second later I thought, why did I wash the blood off? I should have left it there, to let them see what they've done . . . If I'd just had the blood and caked hair when they took the picture . . . I should have kept the blood on."

Everything was ready for the swearing in. But LBJ was still waiting for Jackie. He did not want to proceed without her. Johnson spotted two of JFK's aides and said, "Do you want to ask Mrs. Kennedy if she would like to stand with us?" They hesitated. "She said she wants to be here when I take the oath," the new president told them. "Why don't you see what's keeping her?" Ken O'Donnell went to Jackie, who said, "I think I ought to. In the light of history it would be better if I was there."

She emerged from her room and entered the cabin where Lyndon Johnson, Judge Hughes, the photographer, and a number of the passengers awaited her. Cecil Stoughton had started taking pictures of the scene even before Jackie walked in. Her appearance shocked everyone — they had assumed that she would change into a fresh outfit. Then Johnson took her by the hand and led her to a place at his left side. Lady Bird Johnson stood at her husband's right. Stoughton raised one of his cameras and then, as Judge Hughes read the oath and Johnson repeated it, the photographer took several shots before switching to his second camera. The only other sounds in the cabin were the clicking shutters of the cameras. Jackie's appearance horrified Stoughton, who aimed his lens high to crop off the lower part of her body to hide the bloody skirt and stockings.

It was 2:38 p.m. (CST) when Johnson had raised his right hand and was sworn in as the thirty-sixth president of the United States. It took less than a minute for him to speak the words: "I do solemnly swear that I will faithfully execute the office of President of the United States, and will to the best of my ability, preserve, protect, and defend the Constitution of the

United States. So help me God." Lyndon Johnson had already been president for almost two hours, but when the oath was done, his presidency officially began. And Stoughton had taken what remain, to this day, perhaps the most iconic, riveting, and harrowing photographs in all of American history.

After the swearing in, Jackie returned to the back of the plane, and to the casket. Lyndon Johnson gave an order: "Now, let's get airborne." Before Air Force One left Dallas, Cecil Stoughton hurried off the plane with his cameras and film. It was his job to rush to develop the pictures so that they could be published in the evening newspapers across the country.

Within a few minutes, Air Force One hurtled down the runway and took flight for Washington.

• • •

An alert citizen picked up Lee Harvey Oswald's trail in a commercial district on West Jefferson Boulevard.

When Oswald heard a police siren, he turned his back to the road and pretended to study a display of footwear behind the plate-glass windows of a shoe store. Then, at 1:40 p.m., he ducked inside a movie theater at 231 West Jefferson, sneaking past the ticket seller's window without paying for admission.

He had taken a risk when he hid inside the Texas Theatre. If anyone had followed him there, one telephone call would summon a dozen police cars to the scene. Police departments were, and still are, relentless in pursuing a criminal who has shot one of their own. Even if Oswald had evaded his pursuers, his failure to buy a movie ticket might provoke theater employees to call the police to report a nonpaying customer. Either way, Oswald could find himself trapped inside a building with no

Lyndon Johnson is sworn in as president of the United States aboard Air Force One before it departs Dallas for the nation's capital.

escape. Someone *had* followed Oswald. Johnny Calvin Brewer, manager of Hardy's Shoe Store, found his behavior suspicious, and tracked him to the theater. He persuaded employees to call the police.

Oswald had murdered John Kennedy a little more than an hour ago. Now, he sat in the darkness of a theater watching a matinee showing of a movie about World War II titled *War Is Hell*. The theater was nearly empty. A few men occupied scattered seats. Oswald sat near the back. His prospects were not good. Without money, a car, friends, or accomplices, Oswald had few options. He had already made several key mistakes. He wasted the first precious minutes after he shot the president sitting on a slow-moving city bus. Then he caught a taxi to his rooming house instead of going straight to the bus station where he might catch a bus to Mexico—or anywhere out of Dallas. That mistake led to his disastrous encounter with Officer Tippit. By murdering a policeman, Oswald had provoked a second manhunt. And witnesses could identify him as Tippit's killer. Some of them were chasing him now. What would he do? Where could he go?

Oswald did not enjoy the movie for long. Several police cars pulled up in front of the theater. Detectives ran inside toward the screen and climbed onto the stage. The houselights went on, and a witness identified Oswald. As officers rushed him, Oswald punched one of them in the face and shouted, "This is it!" He reached for his pistol—ready to shoot more policemen. One of them grabbed his arm and twisted the revolver out of his hand. Another punched him. Overpowered, Lee Harvey Oswald gave up.

At 1:50 p.m. (CST), one hour and twenty minutes after the

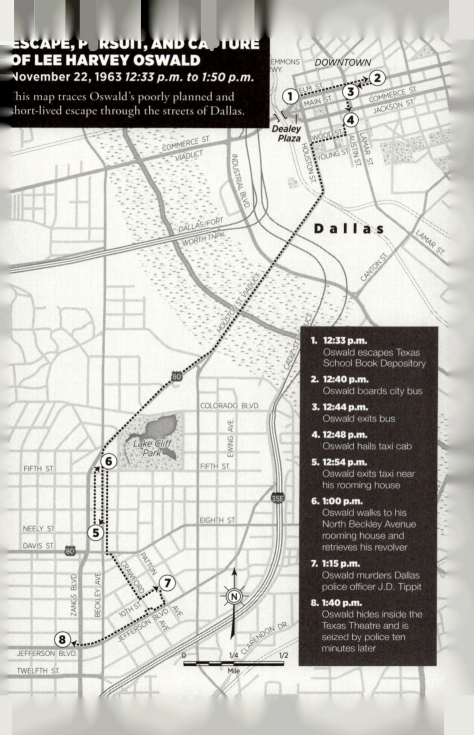

ESCAPE, PURSUIT, AND CAPTURE OF LEE HARVEY OSWALD

November 22, 1963 *12:33 p.m. to 1:50 p.m.*

This map traces Oswald's poorly planned and short-lived escape through the streets of Dallas.

DOWNTOWN

EMMONS FWY.
ELM ST.
MAIN ST.
COMMERCE ST.
JACKSON ST.
Dealey Plaza
COMMERCE ST.
VIADUCT
INDUSTRIAL BLVD.
WOOD ST.
YOUNG ST.
HOUSTON ST.
AUSTIN ST.
LAMAR ST.

DALLAS-FORT WORTH TNPK.

Dallas

LAMAR ST.
CANTON ST.

HOUSTON ST. VIADUCT
CADIZ ST. VIADUCT

COLORADO BLVD.
EWING AVE.
Lake Cliff Park
FIFTH ST.
FIFTH ST.
FIFTH ST.

35E

EIGHTH ST.

NEELY ST.
DAVIS ST.
ZANGS BLVD.
BECKLEY AVE.
CRAWFORD ST.
PATTON AVE.
10TH ST.
JEFFERSON BLVD.
AVE.

JEFFERSON BLVD.
TWELFTH ST.
CLARENDON DR.

N

0   1/4   1/2
Mile

1. **12:33 p.m.**
   Oswald escapes Texas School Book Depository

2. **12:40 p.m.**
   Oswald boards city bus

3. **12:44 p.m.**
   Oswald exits bus

4. **12:48 p.m.**
   Oswald hails taxi cab

5. **12:54 p.m.**
   Oswald exits taxi near his rooming house

6. **1:00 p.m.**
   Oswald walks to his North Beckley Avenue rooming house and retrieves his revolver

7. **1:15 p.m.**
   Oswald murders Dallas police officer J.D. Tippit

8. **1:40 p.m.**
   Oswald hides inside the Texas Theatre and is seized by police ten minutes later

Lee Harvey Oswald as he emerges from the Texas Theatre under arrest, led by detectives and uniformed officers.

president had been shot, his assassin was in custody. The police were not sure that they had caught Kennedy's killer — although they had their suspicions — but they were convinced that they had just apprehended the cold-blooded murderer of Officer Tippit. They shoved their prisoner into a car and drove him to police headquarters, a building not far from the Texas School Book Depository.

• • •

In the back of Air Force One, Jackie Kennedy sat next to her husband's coffin during the entire flight back to Washington, DC. Top aides to John Kennedy took turns visiting Jackie at the back of the plane, where they reminisced and told funny stories of JFK's earlier days in politics and made Jackie laugh. They did not want her to mourn alone.

During the flight, passengers divided into two camps, those who had served President Kennedy, and those who worked for Lyndon Johnson. For the next two hours, uncomfortable tension filled the air. Some Kennedy aides had never liked LBJ. His chief nemesis had been the president's own brother, Attorney General Robert Kennedy, head of the United States Department of Justice. Some of President Kennedy's staffers were snobs who believed that Johnson, who had never attended an elite, Ivy League university as many of them had, was their social and intellectual inferior. Behind his back, they mocked him as a crude country hick from the Texas Hill Country.

In truth, Johnson was a master politician with a record of important achievements. Johnson's earthiness was a mask that often concealed his sophisticated grasp of events and his keen understanding of the minds and behavior of others. Without

Johnson as his vice presidential running mate in 1960, it is unlikely that John Kennedy would ever have been elected president in the first place. In their anguish, some Kennedy staffers now resented Johnson for becoming president. In fact, on November 22, Lyndon Johnson acted with grace and dignity. He did the best he could under the most trying of circumstances.

Forty thousand feet below the jet carrying home the body of John Kennedy and the new President Lyndon Johnson was a stunned nation grieving its fallen leader. By midafternoon, almost everyone in America knew about the assassination. For the rest of their lives, people would remember where they were when they first heard the news that President Kennedy had been shot. On the flight back, Jackie Kennedy began to plan her husband's funeral. Before she was done, she would oversee the biggest, most majestic public funeral in American history since the death of Abraham Lincoln ninety-eight years earlier.

It was dark when, at 6:05 p.m. (EST), Air Force One landed at Andrews Air Force Base outside the nation's capital. Crowds of mourners flocked there to watch the jet land and to see Kennedy's flag-draped coffin removed from the plane. It was not unlike the scene earlier that day when the president landed at Love Field in Dallas. This time the crowd did not cheer. Silence ruled. Television cameras broadcasted live coverage of the event.

The American people were about to get their first look at Jackie Kennedy since the assassination less than five hours ago. A rear door on the plane opened. An elevated platform was put in place to receive the coffin. Then Jackie Kennedy appeared in the doorway. All across the country, millions of people staring at their television screens let out a simultaneous gasp when they

Jacqueline Kennedy watches her husband's coffin as it is carried off Air Force One, as the president's brother Robert holds her hand.

saw the bloodstains on her clothing. Jackie had still not changed out of the clothes she had worn in Dealey Plaza. She wanted Americans to see her pink suit. On television screens, as she walked to the navy ambulance, viewers saw that her legs were smeared with copious amounts of blood. She wanted to sear these images into the collective memory of the American people so that they would never forget. It worked. To this day, decades after the assassination, the mere sight of an image of her in that suit triggers flashbacks in the minds of every person who remembers November 22, 1963.

President Lyndon Johnson strode toward the lights, microphones, and cameras. This time Jackie Kennedy did not accompany him as he made his first public statement as the new president: "This is a sad time for all people. We have suffered a

After Air Force One lands, Lyndon B. Johnson addresses the American people for the first time as their president.

loss that cannot be weighed. For me, it is a deep, personal tragedy. I know the world shares the sorrow that Mrs. Kennedy and her family bear. I will do my best. That is all I can do. I ask for your help—and God's."

On the night of November 22, President Johnson composed two handwritten letters. They were not orders to important U.S. government officials, or communications to world leaders. Instead, LBJ addressed them to the two children who had lost their father. "Dear John," he began his note to JFK's son, "It will be many years before you understand fully what a great man your father was. His loss is a deep personal tragedy for all of us, but I wanted you particularly to know that I share your grief— You can always be proud of him." To the dead president's daughter, he wrote: "Dearest Caroline— Your father's death has been a great tragedy for the Nation, as well as for you at this time. He was a wise and devoted man. You can always be proud of what he did for his country."

• • •

In Dallas, another plane departed Love Field after Air Force One had taken off. It was the cargo plane that had ferried the president's Lincoln Continental limousine to Texas. Secret Service agents had driven the car from Parkland Hospital back to Love Field. At the hospital, an agent removed the two flags— one bearing the presidential seal and the other the American flag—that had hung from the flagpoles on the hood during the motorcade. He handed them to Kennedy's secretary, Evelyn Lincoln. Upon the car's arrival in Washington, agents drove it to the White House garage, where it was hidden from view. Color photographs taken of it there show bloodstains on the

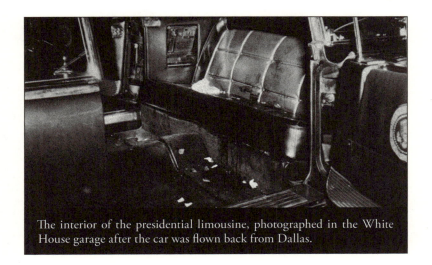

The interior of the presidential limousine, photographed in the White House garage after the car was flown back from Dallas.

two-toned blue leather upholstery. The agents in Dallas had not been able to wash away all the blood.

• • •

From Andrews Air Force Base, President Kennedy was not yet ready to go home to the White House. First, accompanied by Jackie, a navy ambulance took his body to Bethesda Naval Hospital, across the Maryland border from Washington. There would need to be an autopsy to document the official cause of death. Kennedy had been a naval officer, so Jackie, even before Air Force One had touched down, chose Bethesda.

When Jackie entered the hospital, she was taken to a waiting room on the seventeenth floor. As she settled in for a long night, the president's brother Robert told her that a suspect had been arrested for her husband's murder. "They think they found the man who did it," the attorney general said. "He says he's a Communist." Jackie was aghast, and she said to her mother: "He didn't even have the satisfaction of being killed for civil rights . . . It's—it had to be some silly little Communist."

Bethesda Naval Hospital, the president's body was autopsied and embalmed

The president's casket was placed on a cart and wheeled to the room where pathologists and technicians waited to examine him. The autopsy began at 8:00 p.m. (EST). Attendants removed his body, laid him on a table, and unwound the plastic wrapping. They photographed his face, which had been undamaged by the bullets, and his head, which had been ravaged by one. They photographed his neck wound, then rolled him over to photograph his back wound. Then they made X-rays of his skull. Doctors removed what remained of his brain. After examining it, they sealed it in a stainless-steel container with a screw-top lid.

Hours passed, but Jackie Kennedy refused to leave. After the pathologists finished their work, the morticians arrived to prepare the president for burial. Not knowing whether Mrs. Kennedy would choose an open- or closed-coffin viewing before the funeral, the undertakers prepared the president's corpse for an open-coffin viewing. They closed his eyes and sealed them shut. They concealed the tracheotomy cut that the Dallas doctors had sliced in his neck. Then they labored on their most difficult task, reconstructing the side of John Kennedy's skull that the fatal bullet had blown open. A White House courier brought a selection of eight of the president's suits, four pairs of shoes, plus shirts and ties for the morticians to dress him.

They did not finish until after three o'clock in the morning on November 23. Now Jackie could take him home. The ambulance left Bethesda at 3:56 a.m. At the White House, the lights were on and the staff was waiting. At the U.S. Marine Corps barracks at Eighth and I Streets, a contingent of marines awoke from their slumber, donned their dress blue uniforms in record

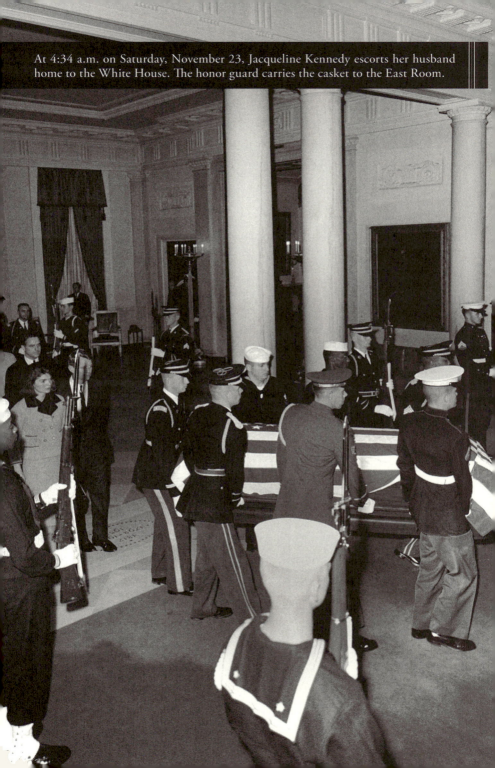

At 4:34 a.m. on Saturday, November 23, Jacqueline Kennedy escorts her husband home to the White House. The honor guard carries the casket to the East Room.

time, and left their barracks for the White House. Flaming torches illuminated their path as they marched through the gate and onto the White House grounds. At 4:34 a.m. (EST), a military honor guard carried the coffin to the East Room, where the body of Abraham Lincoln had once lain in state. It was the first public clue about what kind of funeral Jackie Kennedy had in mind for her husband. Jackie watched the honor guard carry her husband into the East Room. This eerie scene, unfolding in silence in the middle of the night, was sad but touching in its simplicity.

Jackie Kennedy was exhausted. She had been awake for more than twenty hours. She needed rest. The president had been assassinated almost fifteen hours ago. In the morning, she would have much to do, and many decisions to make. For now, she went upstairs to the family suite on the second floor of the White House. There, in the privacy of her bedroom, she undressed, removing her suit, stockings, and other garments stained by the tragedy that she had suffered that day.

SATURDAY
NOVEMBER 23, 1963

Jackie Kennedy awoke in her bedroom at the White House. She had slept only a few hours. Had it really happened? Or had it all been just a nightmare? It was real.

At 8:15 on the morning of Saturday, November 23, she met with her children to talk to them about what had happened. The night before, she had not told Caroline and John the awful news. She knew she would not arrive home before their bedtime, so she deputized their beloved nanny, Maud Shaw, to tell them.

At 10:00 a.m. on the twenty-third, Jackie attended a private mass in the East Room for the president's friends and family. Elsewhere in the White House, staff members were busy cleaning out the Oval Office in the West Wing. A tearful Evelyn Lincoln, John Kennedy's personal secretary since his years in the Senate, gathered papers and personal mementoes from his desk. It was all happening so fast. JFK's famous rocking chairs were removed at 1:31 p.m., loaded onto a handcart, and rolled across a driveway to the Old Executive Office Building, an annex of the White House.

Some of President Kennedy's staffers criticized the new president. It was unseemly and in poor taste, they murmured, for Johnson to move into the White House so quickly. But Lyndon Johnson had not moved into the White House. The West Wing,

Two of President Kennedy's favorite possessions — his rocking chairs — are moved out of the White House soon after the assassination.

which contained the Oval Office, was in a separate building connected to the main White House by a colonnade. A number of officials had advised LBJ to occupy the presidential office at once as a symbol of the continuity of the government. With respect to the White House itself, which contained the historic rooms as well as the president's private living quarters, Johnson was emphatic that Jackie and her children should continue to live there as long as she wished. Mary Todd Lincoln had stayed on in the White House for more than a month after her husband's assassination, and Lyndon Johnson believed that Jackie Kennedy, and not he, should decide when she should move out. He vowed to give her all the time she wanted. But she did not want to stay long.

As Jackie's plans for the funeral evolved, she decided that her husband should be buried at Arlington National Cemetery, a historic graveyard established during the Civil War on General Robert E. Lee's estate, across the Potomac River from the White House. Thousands of soldiers from the Civil War, World War I, World War II, and the Korean War had been buried there. Arlington was also the site of the famous Tomb of the Unknowns. On Saturday afternoon, a little after 2:00 p.m. (EST), Jackie Kennedy arrived at Arlington to inspect and approve the site of the president's grave. It was a lovely spot of ground in front of the old Lee mansion, and it enjoyed a panoramic view of Washington. When John Kennedy had recently visited this spot, he said it was so beautiful that he could stay there forever.

• • •

In Dallas, Lee Harvey Oswald woke up on Saturday, November 23 after his first night in police custody. The previous day, detectives had discovered his loaded rifle, an empty paper bag, and the three spent cartridge cases at the Book Depository. They never found any curtain rods there. Soon, through the unique serial number stamped into the weapon, the FBI would discover records proving that Oswald had ordered it by mail from a sporting goods store in Chicago. The FBI also traced the pistol he had used to shoot J. D. Tippit.

After Oswald's arrest, detectives subjected him to a total of twelve hours of questioning. He was surly, defiant, arrogant, defensive, and self-pitying. He talked a lot, but, unfortunately, the Dallas police department failed to make tape recordings of all of those hours of conversations that detectives had with him on November 22 and in the days that followed. He admitted nothing. He actually seemed to enjoy the attention, and he toyed with the Dallas police, FBI, and Secret Service interrogators. Some notes survive, but they are no substitute for the immediacy and insights that Oswald's own recorded account of himself would have offered. Oswald insisted that he was innocent. He denied shooting President Kennedy or Officer Tippit. He claimed that he did not even own a rifle. Marina Oswald knew better. Later, when she visited Lee at police headquarters, he was calm. He spoke vaguely. He sputtered no outraged proclamations of his innocence. When Marina stared into his eyes, she knew that he had killed the president.

Oswald's wife, Marina, arrives at the Dallas police station.

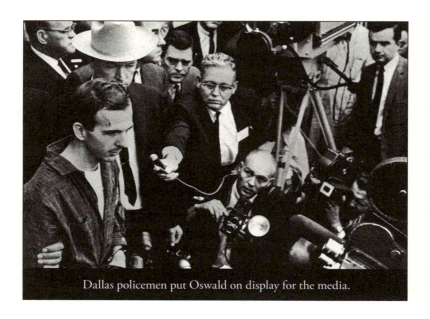
Dallas policemen put Oswald on display for the media.

The Dallas police paraded Oswald before newspaper reporters and television cameras many times. In a crowded hallway, they allowed him to make several public statements that were filmed and broadcast across the country. Oswald played dumb. "I really don't know what this situation is about," he told reporters, "except that I am accused of murdering a policeman. I know nothing more than that." Oswald said he wanted a lawyer. "I do request that someone . . . come forward and give me legal assistance."

When a reporter asked him point-blank, "Did you shoot the president?" Oswald gave an odd, wordy, and indirect reply: "No, I have not been charged with that. In fact, nobody has said that to me yet. The first thing I heard about it was when the newspaper reporters in the hall asked me that question."

The prosecutor discussed the case against Oswald in front of reporters and pronounced him guilty. At one point, Oswald

A defiant Lee Harvey Oswald raises his fist in a clenched salute.

raised his handcuffed hands and, for several seconds, clenched one fist into a Communist salute. Photographs and videos captured the moment. Another time, Oswald complained to journalists that his "fundamental hygienic rights" were being violated because the police would not allow him to take a shower. He told reporters that he had a cut above his eye because a policeman had hit him. He asked for a lawyer several times, but the police and prosecutors ignored him. A policeman walked through a crowded hallway holding Oswald's rifle above his head like a cheap bowling trophy.

The Dallas police department allowed its headquarters to deteriorate into a carnival-like spectacle. Shouting, pushing reporters packed the halls and, like jackals, became frenzied whenever the police teased them with a glimpse of their prisoner. "Oswald, did you shoot the president?" yelled one journalist during one of these brief, impromptu hallway interviews. "I didn't shoot anybody, sir," he replied. "I haven't been told what I am here for." When another reporter shouted the same question, Oswald said, "No, they've taken me in because of the fact that I lived in the Soviet Union." Then Oswald claimed, "I'm just a patsy," by which he meant that he was the fall guy for whoever committed the crime. Oswald admitted just one thing. When asked whether he was in the Book Depository at the time of the assassination, he said yes: "I work in that building . . . naturally, if I work in that building, yes, sir," he was there. But he denied everything else. When a third reporter asked if he was the gunman — "Did you fire that rifle?" — Oswald uttered an emotional denial: "I don't know the facts you people have been given, but I emphatically deny these charges!"

Oswald's rifle is shown off to the media circus crowding the halls at the Dallas police station.

Oswald's denials did not surprise the detectives. Experienced policemen knew that most murderers denied their guilt.

There was no proper security at police headquarters. The wild atmosphere was shameful. No one checked IDs. What explains the incompetence of the police when they had Oswald in their custody? The answer is simple: police officials wanted to curry favor with the journalists from all over the country who had descended upon Dallas. The assassination had stained both the city's and its police department's reputations. There was disturbing talk that the people of Dallas shared some kind of collective guilt for the murder. The police wanted the reporters to say good things about Dallas, so they gave the press free rein. It was a fateful decision that impeded their investigation and put Oswald's life in danger.

• • •

Elsewhere in Dallas on November 23, word had gotten out about Abraham Zapruder's home movie. He had already been interviewed on a local television station. Journalists, desperate to purchase the rights to his film, went to his office to meet with him. He had locked up the film overnight. He hoped to sell it for a lot of money. Soon he would.

• • •

Back at the White House, Jackie Kennedy received important visitors in private after she returned from Arlington Cemetery. Aside from the morning mass, she participated in no other events that day. She needed to conserve her energy in order to gather strength for the ordeal that lay ahead. In two days, on Monday, November 25, she had to be ready to preside over two events that would test her body and soul.

Entrance to the White House draped with black fabric in mourning for the late president.

The first would be her husband's public funeral. With meticulous attention to detail, Jackie Kennedy threw herself into planning the event. With Abraham Lincoln's funeral as her inspiration, researchers had set to work. They uncovered historical details that had been forgotten since the Civil War, including the exact way that the White House entrances and East Room chandeliers had been draped in mourning with ribbons of black crepe paper.

Then, after the funeral, Jackie had to prepare for a second event. On Monday evening, she would host a birthday party for her son, John Jr. In two days, on the day of his father's funeral, he would be three years old. Jackie would not hear of canceling the party.

• • •

All through the day of November 23, and into the night, the body of John F. Kennedy lay in state at the White House.

President John F. Kennedy lies in state in the East Room of the White House.

On Sunday, November 24, Jacqueline Kennedy stood with her children at the north portico of the White House to witness her husband's final departure.

SUNDAY
NOVEMBER 24, 1963

On Sunday, November 24, at 12:34 p.m. (EST), Jackie Kennedy and her brother-in-law Robert entered the East Room and approached the closed, flag-draped coffin. At her request, the honor guard removed the American flag, and the coffin was opened for her. For the last time, she looked upon her husband's face. At 12:37 p.m., she placed two handwritten farewell letters in the coffin. Then it was sealed and again draped with the national colors.

Military pallbearers in immaculate dress uniforms lifted the coffin and carried the late president through the White House and outside to a waiting artillery caisson — a type of wagon — drawn by six gray horses. The soldiers secured the coffin with leather straps. Then, at 1:08 p.m., it left the White House for memorial ceremonies at the U.S. Capitol. Military musicians, the usual crisp *rat-tat-tat* sound of their drums muffled with shrouds of black cloth wrapped around them, beat the mournful sound of the funeral cadence. Formations of troops marched behind the caisson. And tens of thousands of people lined Pennsylvania Avenue. It was just like Abraham Lincoln's funeral procession to the Capitol on April 19, 1865.

At the East Front of the Capitol, the honor guard carried President Kennedy up the steps and past the very spot where, on

President Kennedy leaves the White House for the last time as his body is taken to the U.S. Capitol.

January 20, 1961, he had taken the oath of office. They carried him into the rotunda, and laid his coffin under the Great Dome, upon the very spot where Abraham Lincoln's coffin had once rested. At 2:02 p.m., the Congressional memorial service began. John Kennedy had begun his political career at this place, first as a congressman, then a senator. One of the speakers was Senator Mike Mansfield. His eulogy, a tribute to both John and Jackie Kennedy, stunned listeners. Mansfield recalled the image of how Jackie, at Parkland Hospital, had removed her wedding ring and placed it in her husband's hands:

There was a sound of laughter; in a moment, it was no more. And so she took a ring from her finger and placed it in his hands.

There was a wit in a man neither young nor old, but a wit full of an old man's wisdom and of a child's wisdom, and then, in a moment it was no more. And so she took a ring from her finger and placed it in his hands.

There was a man marked with the scars of his love of country, a body active with the surge of a life far, far from spent and, in a moment, it was no more. And so she took a ring from her finger and placed it in his hands.

There was a father with a little boy, a little girl and a joy of each in the other. In a moment it was no more, and so she took a ring from her finger and placed it in his hands.

There was a husband who asked much and gave much, and out of the giving and the asking wove with a woman what could not be broken in life, and in a moment it was no more. And so she took a ring from her finger and placed it in his hands, and kissed him and closed the lid of a coffin.

President Kennedy's coffin lies in the U.S. Capitol rotunda, beneath the Great Dome that Abraham Lincoln completed during the Civil War.

Jacqueline and her daughter, Caroline, kneel beside JFK's coffin in the rotunda of the U.S. Capitol.

Jackie was awed. Of all the words of tribute spoken and written about President Kennedy, she loved none more. At the conclusion of the ceremony, Jackie and her daughter, Caroline, kneeled by the coffin to say good-bye.

• • •

Simultaneously, fifteen hundred miles away in Dallas, Texas, an act of shocking violence disrupted the solemnity of this day. Thirteen minutes before Jackie Kennedy entered the East Room of the White House, detectives at Dallas police headquarters escorted Lee Harvey Oswald to an elevator that took them down to the underground parking garage. The elevator doors opened, and two detectives, walking with the handcuffed Oswald pinned between them, guided their prisoner toward a waiting vehicle—an armored car—that would transport him to

Police detectives escort Lee Harvey Oswald from the city jail to a vehicle that will transport him to the county jail.

another location. The armored car was a decoy. The police planned to put Oswald in an unmarked car.

For security reasons, the Dallas police should have transferred Oswald in privacy and secrecy. But they could not resist the temptation to announce it in advance and invite the press. When Oswald emerged with the trademark smirk on his face, excited reporters and photographers pressed forward. Two television cameras recorded the scene. Only one, from NBC, was broadcasting live. Then, at 11:21 a.m. (CST) — 12:21 p.m. in the nation's capital — a man in a dark suit emerged from the crowd and took a lunging step toward Oswald. He gripped a revolver in his right hand and pointed it at Oswald's belly. A newspaper photographer froze the moment before the man fired. The gunman fired one shot. A second photographer snapped his shutter a split second after the bullet's impact. Oswald screamed and his body writhed in pain. Oswald collapsed.

A television reporter, Tom Pettit from NBC news, screamed into his microphone. "He's been shot! He's been shot! Lee Oswald has been shot! There's a man with a gun. There's absolute panic, absolute panic here in the basement of the Dallas police headquarters. Detectives have their guns drawn. Oswald has been shot."

Police officers laid him on a gurney. Moments after he had been wounded, Oswald was already unconscious. He was rushed to Parkland Hospital, where some of the same people who treated President Kennedy now tried to save the life of his suspected assassin. Out of respect for the president, they did not treat Oswald in the same emergency room where Kennedy had

Lee Harvey Oswald recoils in pain the instant after he is shot by Jack Ruby (in the dark suit on the right).

The wounded Oswald lies on a stretcher.

died. But it was too late. The bullet had penetrated several vital organs, and Oswald had suffered a massive loss of blood. Without regaining consciousness, without speaking any last words, and without confessing his crime, Lee Harvey Oswald died at 2:07 p.m. (EST), just after President Kennedy's memorial at the Capitol had begun.

NBC had broadcast the murder of Oswald on live television to the entire nation. The assassin's assassin was a man named Jack Rubenstein, or Jack Ruby, as he was known. He was a middle-aged club owner and a creature from a world of sleazy nightlife, where men drank stiff drinks and paid women to dance for them onstage. He, like Oswald, was another fringe character, an impulsive, moody, and violent man and, even more than Oswald, given to wild, unstable emotional swings. Ruby thought he would be a hero.

It was unwholesome, almost profane, that for the rest of the day, news coverage of the shooting of Lee Harvey Oswald interrupted news coverage of John F. Kennedy's memorial events.

• • •

The service at the Capitol came to an end. Now the American people would have their turn to pay homage to the fallen president. The bronze doors of the East Front were thrown open to all comers who wanted to view the coffin. Tens of thousands of people were already in line. By 8:00 p.m., two hundred thousand stood in a line that stretched all the way down East Capitol Street and, twelve blocks away, past Lincoln Park, where a bronze sculpture of the Great Emancipator — Abraham Lincoln — beckoned a freed slave to rise. Beyond the park, the line seemed limitless. At 9:04 p.m., Jackie and Robert Kennedy made a surprise return visit to the rotunda. Then they walked outside, among the crowd, and along Constitution Avenue for a while before they returned to the White House. In the darkness — and because it seemed unimaginable that Jackie Kennedy would walk among them — almost no one recognized her.

MONDAY
NOVEMBER 25, 1963

At 2:00 a.m. (EST) on Monday, November 25, the line to get into the Capitol was three miles long. By 9:00 a.m., two hundred and fifty thousand people had filed past the coffin. There was no more time to admit everyone else still standing in the long line. People who had waited for hours were turned away. Now it was time for the president's funeral. Jacqueline Kennedy could have remained at the White House while her husband's coffin was removed from the Capitol and brought to the mansion. But she went to get him.

Since 12:30 p.m. (CST) on Friday, November 22, she had accompanied her husband wherever he went: on the high-speed race from Dealey Plaza to Parkland Hospital; on the ride with the coffin from Parkland to Love Field; aboard Air Force One for the flight home to Washington; in the hearse to Bethesda Naval Hospital, and from there the twilight motorcade home to the White House, and the East Room; the Pennsylvania Avenue procession to the U.S. Capitol; and now, President Kennedy's parting from the Congress he loved. Wherever he went, she followed, until she would take him to the place where she could follow no more.

Her limousine arrived at the Capitol at around 10:40 a.m. Jackie, escorted by the president's two brothers, ascended the

A huge crowd gathers at the U.S. Capitol while the body of President Kennedy rests inside.

steps and walked into the rotunda. She knelt before the coffin and prayed. Then the military casket team lifted the coffin from the catafalque, carried it out of the rotunda, and descended the stairs to the East Front. They strapped it to the caisson. At 11:00 a.m., the cortege departed the Capitol for the White House. From there, starting at 11:35 a.m., Jacqueline Kennedy led a procession on foot to Saint Matthew's Cathedral, eight blocks away. Many heads of state from around the world—kings, presidents, prime ministers, and more—plus distinguished diplomats, had traveled to Washington for the event. Most, unless they were too old or too frail, walked to the cathedral. The Secret Service begged Lyndon Johnson to ride in a car and not march in the procession—it was too dangerous, they warned, and they did not want to lose another president. Johnson refused: "I would rather give my life than be afraid to give it."

On Monday, November 25, a caisson drawn by six horses carried President Kennedy's body from the U.S. Capitol to the funeral at Saint Matthew's Cathedral.

At 12:15 p.m., the pallbearers carried the flag-draped coffin into Saint Matthew's. More than one thousand people attended the service, a low mass conducted by the famous Catholic priest Richard Cardinal Cushing of Boston. The hour-long service confused John Jr. He fidgeted and asked, "Where's my daddy?" The sacred music, the religious incantations, and the somber setting proved too much for Jackie. She could no longer hold it in. She began to cry uncontrollably. Her sobbing body heaved and shook.

At the end of the mass, Cushing said: "May the angels, dear Jack, lead you into Paradise. May the martyrs receive you at your coming. May the spirit of God embrace you, and mayest thou, with all those who made the supreme sacrifice of dying for others, receive eternal rest and peace."

Jackie thought his voice sounded like "a plea, almost a wail." That phrase, "May the angels, dear Jack . . ." unleashed in her fresh spasms of emotion and she began to sob and shake again. Her daughter, Caroline, took her hand and said: "You'll be all right, Mummy. Don't cry. I'll take care of you."

After the service, Jacqueline Kennedy and her children, standing outside the cathedral, watched the honor guard carry the coffin down the steps. A military band played "Hail to the Chief." Jackie bent down and whispered into her little boy's ear: "John, you can salute Daddy now and say good-bye to him." John Kennedy Jr. stepped forward and saluted his father's coffin—just like he had seen the soldiers in uniform do. It was a heartbreaking gesture that became one of the most unforgettable images of the tragedy.

John Jr. salutes his father to say good-bye.

At 1:30 p.m., the horse-drawn caisson bearing President Kennedy departed Saint Matthew's for Arlington Cemetery. It took one hour and fifteen minutes to get there. At a brief grave-side service, a bugler played taps. He was so emotional that he played a wrong note. A formation of fifty fighter jets screamed overhead. In a stunning tribute, the presidential jet, Air Force One, descended to an altitude of five hundred feet above the cemetery and dipped its wings in tribute while it whooshed past at six hundred miles per hour. Artillery cannon fired a twenty-one-gun salute, and riflemen fired three volleys overhead.

The funeral procession crosses Memorial Bridge on the way to the president's gravesite at Arlington National Cemetery.

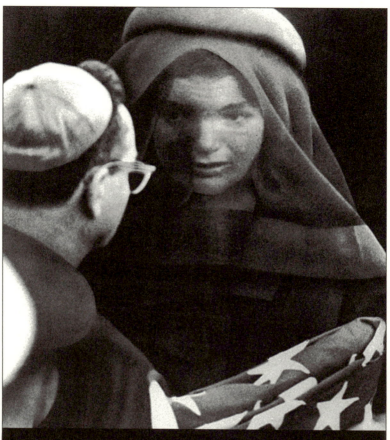

At the graveside, Jackie holds the folded American flag that had earlier covered her husband's coffin.

Soldiers removed the flag from the coffin, folded it into a triangle, and presented it to Jackie.

At 3:13 p.m., Jacqueline Kennedy used a taper to light an "eternal flame" beside the grave. Two days ago she had made a last-minute request. She said that at the climax of the service at Arlington, she wanted to light a flame that would burn forever in memory of her husband. She recalled the day when she and the president had toured the Civil War battlefield of Gettysburg.

There, at the Eternal Light Peace Memorial, dedicated by President Franklin Roosevelt in 1938, she had seen an eternal flame — a gas-powered fire that burned day and night, around the clock — that illuminated the top of the tall monument. At Arlington, army engineers had one built at ground level next to President Kennedy's gravesite in less than twenty-four hours, and it was ready in time for Jackie to light it on Monday afternoon.

She got into her limousine. She wanted to return to the White House, where she planned to greet the funeral guests, especially foreign leaders and diplomats who had come from faraway places. But after leaving Arlington, her car pulled away from the rest of the motorcade. It drove on alone to the Lincoln Memorial, where Jackie looked through the window and gazed up at the sculpture of Father Abraham, who had perished from an assassin's bullet ninety-eight years ago. The sight of Lincoln comforted her.

• • •

Far from Washington, there were other funerals this day. In Texas, Dallas police officer J. D. Tippit was buried with full honors — more than one thousand people attended the service.

Also that afternoon, Lee Harvey Oswald was buried in a cheap cloth-covered pine casket. The timing was shocking — it was the same day as the funerals for the two men he murdered, President Kennedy and Officer Tippit. At Oswald's hurried, ten-minute graveside ceremony, more than seventy-five reporters, photographers, and law enforcement officials far outnumbered the handful of mourners.

Aside from his family, no one who knew him wanted to be

seen at his funeral. No friends came forward to serve as pallbearers. Reporters volunteered to carry the assassin's lonely casket. The minister who promised to officiate failed to show up. Only Oswald's family—his wife, Marina, and their two daughters; his mother, Marguerite; and his brother Robert came to mourn him. *Life* magazine published photographs of the funeral, including a large, double-page image taken at dusk that made it appear that heaven itself—with dark, gloomy, and threatening skies—had cursed Oswald in the grave. That night, watchmen stood guard over the assassin's final resting place to prevent distraught citizens from, under the cover of darkness, desecrating the grave.

• • •

That night at the White House, at 7:00 p.m., Jacqueline Kennedy hosted a little birthday party for her son. He was now three years old.

Then, later in the evening, Robert Kennedy asked Jackie, "Should we go visit our friend?"

"Oh yes," she said.

At midnight, after everyone had gone, she returned to Arlington Cemetery to bid her husband a private and final farewell. By now the casket had been lowered into the grave and covered with a mound of earth. It was quiet now. The eternal flame flickered and danced in the dark. The glow cast streaks of light and shadow across Jackie's face.

• • •

It was done. Four days of blood and death, of mourning and drums, were over. America would never be the same.

The eternal flame burns next to President Kennedy's grave the night of his funeral, November 25, 1963. The Lee Mansion stands majestically in the background.

Artist Bill Mauldin's iconic newspaper cartoon of the sculpture at the Lincoln Memorial weeping at the death of President Kennedy. It became world famous and forever linked the two assassinated presidents.

EPILOGUE

Two days after the funeral, on November 27, 1963, President Lyndon Johnson addressed a joint session of Congress. "All I have I would have given gladly not to be standing here today. The greatest leader of our time has been struck down by the foulest deed of our time. Today John Kennedy lives on in the immortal words and works that he left behind. He lives on in the mind and memories of mankind. He lives in the hearts of his countrymen. . . . An assassin's bullet has thrust upon me the awesome burden of the presidency. . . . I profoundly hope that the tragedy and the torment of these terrible days will bind us together in new fellowship, making us one people in our hour of sorrow. So let us here highly resolve that John Fitzgerald Kennedy did not live — or die — in vain." The new president vowed to carry on the dead president's work.

On November 29, Johnson appointed a special presidential commission, chaired by Chief Justice of the United States Earl Warren, to "study and report upon all facts and circumstances relating to the assassination of the late president, John F. Kennedy, and the subsequent and violent death of the man charged with the assassination." LBJ instructed the special commission to "satisfy itself that the truth is known as far as can be discovered, and to report its findings to him, to the American people, and to the world."

On December 6, Jacqueline Kennedy moved out of the White House and returned to her beloved Georgetown. She wanted to live a quiet life. But now she was an American hero. People mailed eight hundred thousand condolence letters to her. Her home became a tourist attraction. Photographers began to stalk her. Magazines would not stop publishing articles about her. She had become an obsession. So, less than a year after the assassination, in an effort to reclaim her private life, Jacqueline Kennedy abandoned Washington, never to live there again.

In January 1964, before moving away, she appeared in a short film — it was less than three minutes long — to thank the American people for their condolences and expressions of love for her husband. She thanked them for their letters, promised that they would be archived at the Kennedy Library, and said all the usual niceties one might expect a widow in her position to say. Then she caught viewers off guard with an emotional and revealing statement. In the middle of her remarks, she paused and said: "All his bright light gone from the world."

• • •

Ten months after the assassination, on September 24, 1964, the Warren Commission completed the report of its investigation. Almost three hundred thousand words long, the report was accompanied by twenty-six volumes, totaling seventeen thousand pages of testimony, photographs, and exhibits. Its central finding was that Lee Harvey Oswald had assassinated John F. Kennedy, that two of the three shots he fired had struck the president, that the assassin had acted alone, and that there was no evidence that he was part of a conspiracy.

Many people found it hard to believe that such an

At the White House, Chief Justice Earl Warren presents a copy of the Warren Report to President Lyndon B. Johnson.

inconsequential man as Oswald could change history in such a monumental way. Many thought, and still think, that this crime was too great to be explained by random chance. They wanted a more profound and complicated explanation. This was not unusual. For more than two centuries, Americans have turned to numerous conspiracy theories to explain catastrophic events or troubled times. In the 1960s, many found Oswald's journey to the Soviet Union and his interest in Cuba suspicious. Was his murder just two days after the assassination a coincidence? Or was there a plot to silence him?

These and other questions provoked some critics to doubt the conclusions in the Warren Report, and to question even the most simple, obvious, and persuasive evidence of Oswald's guilt. Many of the conspiracy theorists have devoted their lives to trying to prove that John F. Kennedy was the victim of one plot or another. Many of their theories—and there are a dizzying number of them—contradict one another. According to the most popular ones, the president was killed by: a Russian or Cuban Communist conspiracy; the anti-Communist American "right wing"; organized crime—the Mafia; the CIA; the FBI; the U.S. military; Texas millionaires in the oil business; the "military-industrial complex"; or even Vice President Lyndon Johnson.

Some conspiracy theorists claim that Oswald fired no shots in Dealey Plaza. They argue—despite the convincing evidence against him—that he was framed. Others admit that Oswald fired the shots but insist that he was not the lone gunman, and that additional snipers—two, three, four, or more—fired as many as sixteen rounds, even though most witnesses said they heard only three. One theory asserts that there were two Oswalds—the real one, and the other an imposter. A few critics even accuse JFK's Secret Service agents, the U.S. Navy doctors at Bethesda Naval Hospital, and even Dallas police officer J. D. Tippit of being part of the conspiracy.

Some of the theories rely on falsified evidence. Others are based on lies. Some theorists believe that the same master conspiracy behind the Kennedy assassination controls other important events in American life. But all the theories have one thing in common. They reject the proven role that chance, luck, randomness, coincidence, or mistake have played in human history for thousands of years.

This much can be said. No one, after all these years, has yet disproved the key conclusion of the Warren Commission: Lee Harvey Oswald was the assassin, and he acted alone. Just as the conspiracy theorists have questioned the evidence of the assassination, so must a reader question their writings with equal skepticism. Today we know much more about the assassination of President Kennedy than the members of the Warren Commission did. More information and more sophisticated advances in science and technology have illuminated the crime and its evidence in new ways. But as of now, no new research or analysis has overturned the verdict of the Warren Commission. Indeed, in the future — fifty or one hundred years from now — it is more likely that the discovery of any new evidence, along with further scientific discoveries, will only strengthen the case against Lee Harvey Oswald.

• • •

One great mystery remains: Why? Why did Oswald assassinate John F. Kennedy? Lee never told his wife, mother, or brother when they visited him in jail. He never told the Dallas police, the Secret Service, or the FBI when they questioned him. Perhaps, embittered, he killed the president to impress Soviet officials who placed so little value on him after his defection. But by the fall of 1963, Lee had long soured on life in Russia and had renounced the corruptions of Soviet Communism. Could he have wanted to impress Fidel Castro and seek political asylum in Cuba, fantasizing that he would become a revolutionary hero? Or, could it be possible that Oswald came under the influence of others, not as a paid assassin or the agent of a conspiracy, but as someone who listened to whisperings in his ear telling him that any man who killed a president would go down in history?

Perhaps his motive was not politics but fame. As long as the world remembered John Kennedy, it could never forget the man who murdered him. Or maybe Oswald was one of America's first glory killers, obsessed with JFK's glamorous, movie star–like celebrity. By killing the president, Oswald's deluded mind sought to merge their identities, hoping that some of the JFK magic that Oswald never possessed — effervescence, popularity, success, and even greatness — might rub off on him. Oswald longed to possess the traits that were never meant to be his. Or, in the end, perhaps the reason is much more simple and fundamental, and lies beyond rational human understanding: Lee Harvey Oswald was evil.

It is impossible to know. Whatever his motives, Oswald took them with him to the grave. If he could return today to the scene of his crime, he would be pleased to see that, half a century later, he remains the subject of endless fascination and speculation. He taunts us still, defying us to solve the mystery of the *why* that he left behind. Unlike John Wilkes Booth, the assassin of Abraham Lincoln, Lee Harvey Oswald did not leap to the stage, boast of his crime, and wave a bloody dagger before our eyes. No, Oswald struck from the shadows. Then he robbed us of the rest of the story. The assassination of President John F. Kennedy in Dallas, Texas, on November 22, 1963, is as compelling as any drama written by William Shakespeare. It is the great American tragedy. Except for this: The tale is incomplete. In the tragedy that he wrote, Lee Oswald left the stage before the final act. He quit the drama before the play was done, and before he told us why he did it or how the story would end.

• • •

John F. Kennedy's unfinished life was cut short before he could fulfill his potential. He was just forty-six years old. The nation mourned the death of its young president, not only for the loss of what he had been — but also for the loss of what he might have become. JFK loved America. He was an optimist about the country's future. He had shown signs of greatness. If he had lived and won reelection in 1964, he would have served until January 20, 1969. One can only speculate about what he might have accomplished if he had more time.

Many people, especially those who lived through it, see the Kennedy assassination as a dividing line in our history, and November 22, 1963, as the day when something went terribly wrong in American life. They believe that the murder ushered in a dark era and set in motion a series of awful events: the escalation of the Vietnam War; civil unrest; racial violence; and, five years later, the assassinations of Martin Luther King Jr. and of the late president's own brother, Robert Kennedy. We can look back and wonder, but we will never know the ways in which the death of John F. Kennedy altered the future course of American history.

• • •

Reflecting on her husband's life, Jacqueline Kennedy said: "I realized that history was what made Jack what he was. You must think of him as this little boy, sick so much of the time, reading in bed, reading the knights of the Round Table. . . . For Jack, history was full of heroes. And if it made him this way — if it made him see the heroes — maybe other little boys will see."

She recognized that the assassination had transformed him

into a hero too: "Now, I think I should have known that he was magic all along — but I should have guessed that it would be too much to ask to grow old with [him] and see our children grow up together. So now, he is a legend when he would have preferred to be a man."

Jackie contemplated the meaning of his life: "John Kennedy believed so strongly that one's aim should not just be the most comfortable life possible — but that we should all do something to right the wrongs we see — and not just complain about them. We owe that to our country . . .

"He believed," Jacqueline Kennedy said, "that one man can make a difference — and that every man should try."

• • •

In Georgetown, the house from which John and Jacqueline Kennedy set out on the journey that began on January 20, 1961, and ended on November 22, 1963, still stands. Over the last half century, little about it has changed. If you go there today, perhaps on a chilly fall evening late in November, when the crisp, fallen leaves crinkle underfoot, the twin lamps beside the front door still burn, still glowing in the darkness of the night.

DIAGRAMS, PHOTOS, AND ILLUSTRATIONS

It is an old cliché that "one picture is worth a thousand words," but in the case of the assassination of President Kennedy, that timeworn saying is true. The following diagrams, photos, and artworks illustrate several key elements of the story of November 22, 1963. Three diagrams show the location of Lee Harvey Oswald's sniper's nest on the sixth floor of the Texas School Book Depository, explain the step-by-step operation of his bolt action rifle, and reveal how he escaped from the Book Depository within three minutes of shooting the president. Two additional diagrams depict the angles of the three shots fired at the presidential limousine and trace their flight paths back to the Book Depository. They show how President Kennedy and Governor Connally were seated in positions that allowed one bullet to strike and pass through both men. Other images indicate where two bullets struck the president, and show that the bullet that hit both the president and the governor did not survive in pristine condition, but was deformed by the impact. Together, these artworks illustrate some of the key evidence that shows how Lee Harvey Oswald could—and did—assassinate President John F. Kennedy.

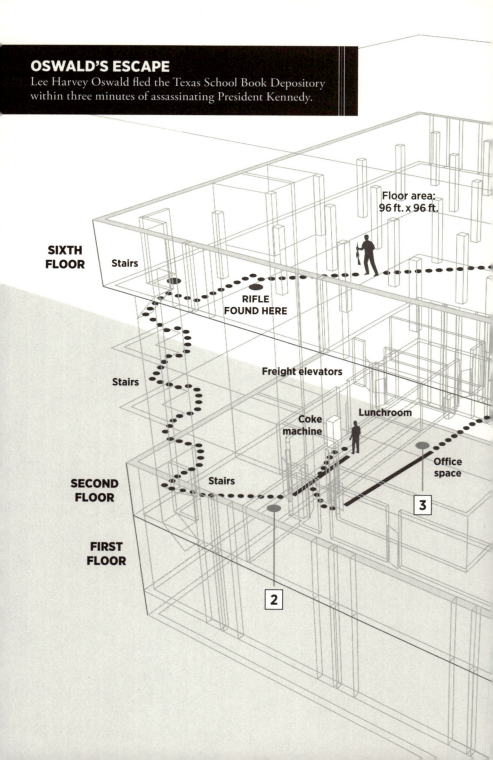

OSWALD'S ESCAPE

Lee Harvey Oswald fled the Texas School Book Depository within three minutes of assassinating President Kennedy.

Floor area:
96 ft. x 96 ft.

SIXTH FLOOR

Stairs

RIFLE FOUND HERE

Stairs

Freight elevators

Coke machine

Lunchroom

Stairs

Office space

SECOND FLOOR

3

FIRST FLOOR

2

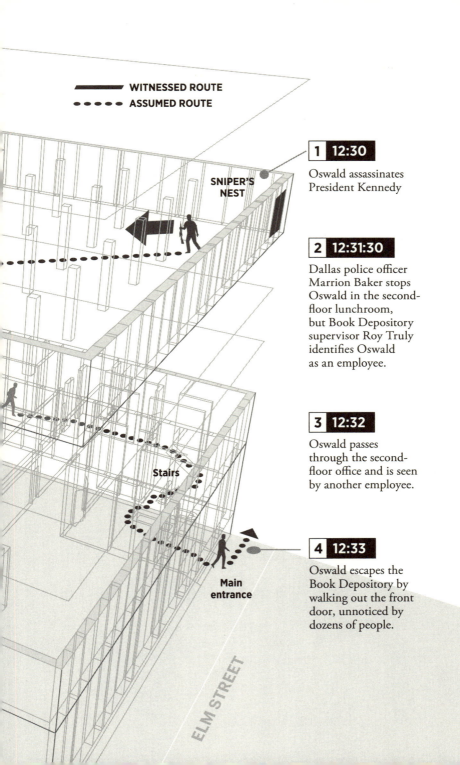

WITNESSED ROUTE

ASSUMED ROUTE

SNIPER'S NEST

Stairs

Main entrance

ELM STREET

1 **12:30**

Oswald assassinates President Kennedy

2 **12:31:30**

Dallas police officer Marrion Baker stops Oswald in the second-floor lunchroom, but Book Depository supervisor Roy Truly identifies Oswald as an employee.

3 **12:32**

Oswald passes through the second-floor office and is seen by another employee.

4 **12:33**

Oswald escapes the Book Depository by walking out the front door, unnoticed by dozens of people.

Oswald could operate the bolt to eject a fired cartridge and reload a new one in less than a second.

1. Push bolt up... **2.** Pull back (to eject case and position next cartridge)... **3.** Push forward...
4. Push down (to lock bolt).

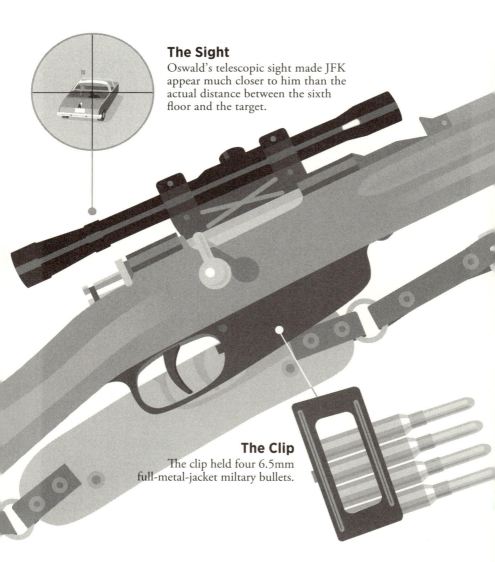

The Sight
Oswald's telescopic sight made JFK appear much closer to him than the actual distance between the sixth floor and the target.

The Clip
The clip held four 6.5mm full-metal-jacket miltary bullets.

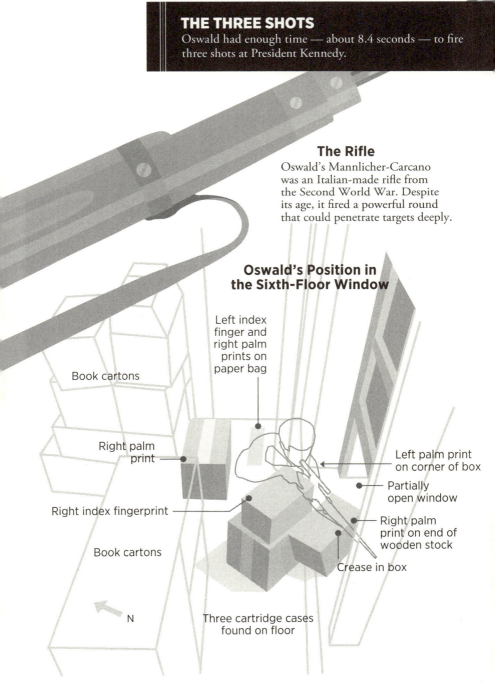

The Rifle

Oswald's Mannlicher-Carcano was an Italian-made rifle from the Second World War. Despite its age, it fired a powerful round that could penetrate targets deeply.

Oswald's Position in the Sixth-Floor Window

Left index finger and right palm prints on paper bag

Book cartons

Right palm print

Right index fingerprint

Book cartons

Left palm print on corner of box

Partially open window

Right palm print on end of wooden stock

Crease in box

N

Three cartridge cases found on floor

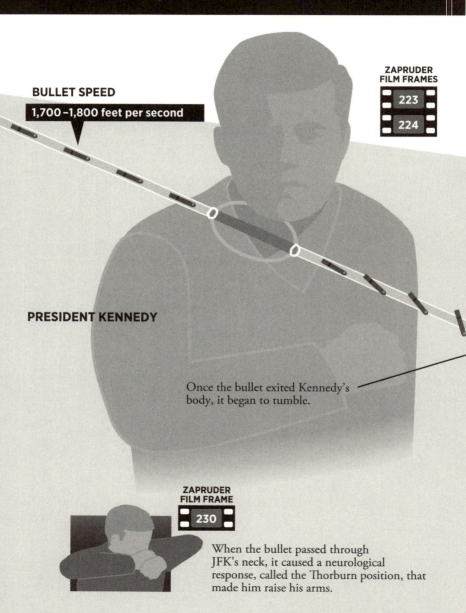

THE SINGLE BULLET

The bullet from Oswald's second shot passed through the upper bodies of both JFK and Governor Connally. Governor Connally sat to the left and slightly lower than the president. The bullet was deflected when it hit Connally's rib. It entered his right wrist, then his left thigh.

ZAPRUDER FILM FRAMES
223
224

BULLET SPEED
1,700 –1,800 feet per second

PRESIDENT KENNEDY

Once the bullet exited Kennedy's body, it began to tumble.

ZAPRUDER FILM FRAME
230

When the bullet passed through JFK's neck, it caused a neurological response, called the Thorburn position, that made him raise his arms.

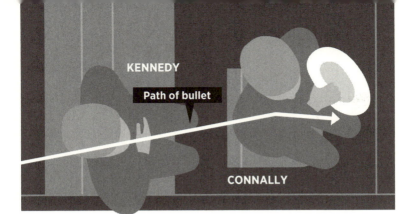

KENNEDY

Path of bullet

CONNALLY

▲

GOVERNOR CONNALLY

1,500–1,600 feet per second

The tumbling bullet struck
Connally's right shoulder.

The bullet passed
through the governor's
body and broke one
of his ribs.

The bullet exited
the right side of
Connally's chest.

900 feet per second

Then, traveling backward,
the bullet fractured his wrist.

The bullet lodged in Connally's
thigh just below the skin.

400 feet per second

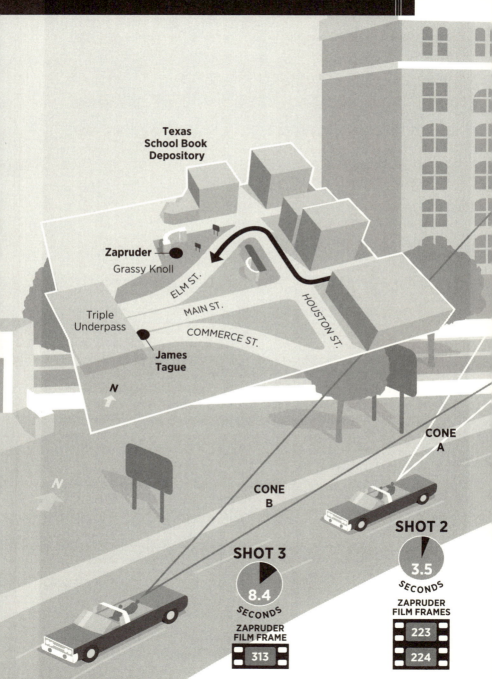

DIAGRAM OF OSWALD'S THREE SHOTS AT JFK

Texas School Book Depository

Zapruder

Grassy Knoll

ELM ST.

MAIN ST.

Triple Underpass

COMMERCE ST.

HOUSTON ST.

James Tague

N

CONE A

CONE B

SHOT 2

3.5 SECONDS

ZAPRUDER FILM FRAMES

223

224

SHOT 3

8.4 SECONDS

ZAPRUDER FILM FRAME

313

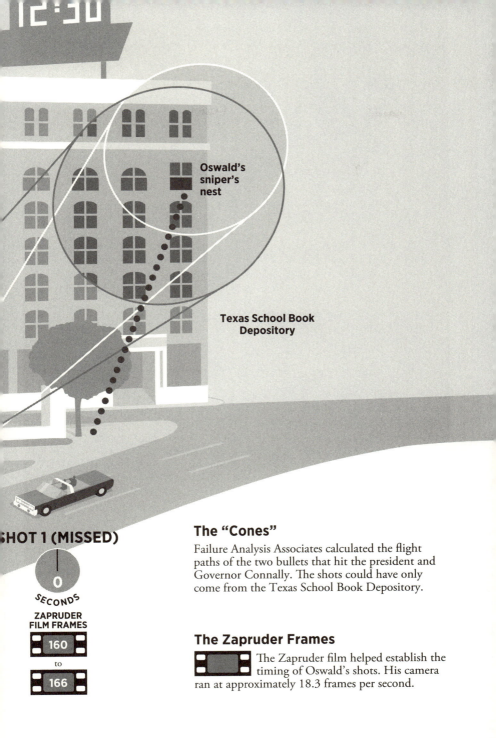

Oswald's sniper's nest

Texas School Book Depository

SHOT 1 (MISSED)

0

SECONDS

ZAPRUDER
FILM FRAMES

160

to

166

The "Cones"

Failure Analysis Associates calculated the flight paths of the two bullets that hit the president and Governor Connally. The shots could have only come from the Texas School Book Depository.

The Zapruder Frames

The Zapruder film helped establish the timing of Oswald's shots. His camera ran at approximately 18.3 frames per second.

CE 399

FBI C1

National Archives

TOP: Side view of the bullet that struck President Kennedy and Governor Connally. BOTTOM: Rear-end view of the same bullet, showing how it was deformed from impact.

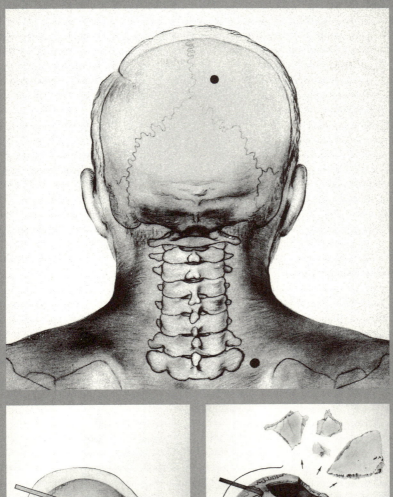

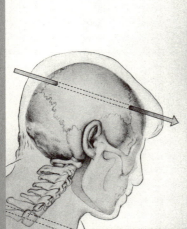

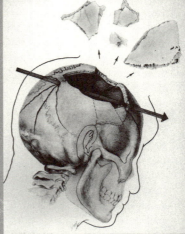

Artistic depictions of President Kennedy's wounds. These drawings show where the second and third bullets entered the president.

PLACES TO VISIT

Today you can visit many of the places that you have read about in *"The President Has Been Shot!"* In Dallas, the Texas School Book Depository still stands at the corner of Elm and Houston Streets. The building was fortunate to survive the assassination of President Kennedy. Ashamed that the murder happened in their city, and humiliated that their police department had allowed Oswald to be shot right under their noses, many citizens of Dallas wanted the Book Depository to be torn down. To them, it was an ugly landmark of the day that Dallas could never forget, and that they feared would scar the city's image forever. But cooler heads prevailed, and the Book Depository was preserved for history. It no longer serves as a warehouse for textbooks. Like Ford's Theatre in Washington, where John Wilkes Booth assassinated Abraham Lincoln, the Texas School Book Depository is now a museum.

Today, an institution named the Sixth Floor Museum occupies the place that Lee Harvey Oswald made infamous. Once a controversial and unwelcome reminder of Dallas's shame, today the museum is an important part of the city's cultural landscape that has attracted millions of visitors. It is not a shrine to Lee Harvey Oswald, and it does not sensationalize the crime. Instead, it is a responsible museum that frames the events in

Dallas within the larger context of JFK's life story, American politics, and the culture of 1960s America. The museum honors John F. Kennedy, not his assassin. What a mistake it would have been, fifty years ago in the heat of passion, to have torn the building down.

Like Oswald did many times, you can take an elevator to the sixth floor and there retrace his footsteps to the wall of windows facing Elm Street. But you can no longer gaze out the window from which he shot the president. To protect the sniper's nest from vandals and souvenir hunters, a Plexiglas barrier now surrounds Oswald's window. You can, however, stand at the window next to it, look down to the street, and imagine what Oswald must have seen on the afternoon of November 22, 1963.

In Dallas, there are other things to see: Oswald's escape route from the Book Depository to his rooming house, from there to the street where he shot police officer J. D. Tippit, and from there to the place of his capture at the Texas Theatre. There is another sight to see, the haunted place where on the night of Thursday, November 21, or early on the morning of Friday, November 22, Lee Harvey Oswald decided to carry out his plan: Ruth Paine's house, still a private home, where Oswald slept on the eve of the assassination, and from which he emerged the next morning with his rifle, determined to kill a president.

In Washington, DC, several places evoke the presence of John F. Kennedy. The Georgetown house at 3307 N Street NW survives as a private home. A few blocks away, on Wisconsin Avenue, the venerable bar and restaurant Martin's Tavern still serves meals to customers just as it did to Lyndon B. Johnson,

Richard M. Nixon, and a young, unmarried Senator John F. Kennedy. When Kennedy dined there alone, he often sat at the first table to the right after walking through the door—the half booth or "rumble seat," with a bench on only one side of the table. Legend has it that he proposed to Jackie Bouvier at another window booth in the restaurant.

Also in Georgetown are the former W. Averell Harriman house at 3038 N Street NW, where Jackie moved after she left the White House in December 1963, and the second house she moved to, at 3017 N Street NW. If you are lucky enough to enjoy a White House tour that includes a visit to the East Room, pause and imagine President Kennedy's flag-draped coffin lying there. If you visit the United States Capitol, stand at the center of the rotunda, below the Great Dome, and imagine two hundred and fifty thousand mourners walking past the spot. At Arlington National Cemetery, just outside Washington, DC, you can visit President Kennedy's grave and see the eternal flame that still burns there. And if you go to Gettysburg, Pennsylvania, a ninety-minute drive from the nation's capital, you can visit the Eternal Light Peace Memorial that John and Jackie Kennedy viewed during their March 1963 battlefield tour, and you can see the eternal flame that inspired her to create one for her fallen husband.

To learn more about John Kennedy's life, visit his presidential library in Boston, which has many fine and educational exhibits. There the focus is on how he lived, not on how he died. Outside of Boston, in Brookline, Massachusetts, you can visit JFK's birthplace home, where his journey began, and now a U.S.

National Park Service site. Inside the house, a tape-recorded interview with his mother recalling his early years plays over hidden speakers, which brings the home to life. In the otherwise quiet rooms, you can feel the presence of young John Kennedy, long before history claimed him.

SOURCE NOTES

PROLOGUE

JFK's homes in Georgetown — John F. Kennedy lived in several homes in Georgetown from the time he first came to Washington, DC, after being elected to the U.S. House of Representatives in 1946. All these properties are still standing and can be viewed on a walking tour. See the DC Traveler's web page for "A Tour of JFK's Camelot" at www.thedctraveler.com/2007/01/a-tour-of-jfks-camelot/. For photographs of the Kennedys in Georgetown, see: Mark Shaw, *The John F. Kennedys: A Family Album.* New York: Rizzoli, 2000 (revised edition). Orlando Suero, and Anne Garside. *Camelot at Dawn: Jacqueline and John Kennedy in Georgetown, May 1954.* Baltimore: Johns Hopkins University Press, 2001.

PART ONE: INTRODUCTION TO JOHN F. KENNEDY

JFK's father — For an early comprehensive biography on Joseph P. Kennedy and his desire for one of his sons to become president, see: Richard J. Whalen, *The Founding Father: The Story of Joseph P. Kennedy.* New York: New American Library, 1964. For a more recent biography, see: David Nasaw, *The Patriarch: The Remarkable Life and Turbulent Times of Joseph P. Kennedy.* New York: Penguin, 2012.

PT-109 — For a readable account of the PT-109 incident, see: Robert J. Donovan, *PT 109: John F. Kennedy in World War II.* New York: McGraw-Hill, 1961. See also: Edward J. Renehan Jr., *The Kennedys at War: 1937–1945.* New York: Doubleday, 2002; Nigel Hamilton, *JFK: Reckless Youth.* New York: Random House, 1992.

JFK's wedding — A brief summary of the wedding details can be found on the John F. Kennedy Library and Museum website: www.jfklibrary.org/Research/Ready-Reference/JBKO-Miscellaneous-Information/Wedding-Details.aspx. See also: C. David Heymann, *A Woman Named Jackie: An Intimate Biography of Jacqueline Bouvier Kennedy Onassis.* Secaucus, NJ: Carol Communications, 1989; Sarah Bradford, *America's Queen: The Life of Jacqueline Kennedy Onassis.* New York: Viking, 2000; Edward Klein, *All Too Human: The Love Story of Jack and Jackie Kennedy.* New York: Pocket Books, 1996.

Kennedy versus Nixon—There have been many books comparing and contrasting John Kennedy to Richard Nixon. There was even a politically motivated work published during the 1960 election. See: Arthur M. Schlesinger Jr., *Kennedy or Nixon: Does It Make Any Difference?* New York: Macmillan, 1960.

Kennedy-Nixon TV debates—See: Sidney Kraus, ed., *The Great Debates: Background, Perspective, Effects.* Bloomington: Indiana University Press, 1962. See also: Newton N. Minow, and Craig L. LaMay. *Inside the Presidential Debates: Their Improbable Past and Promising Future.* Chicago: University of Chicago Press, 2008. The first one-hour televised debate can be viewed on the United Press International (UPI) website, at www.upi.com/blog/2012/10/03/Watch-the-full-Kennedy-Nixon-debate-from-1960/4461349300140

Inaugural address—See: *Public Papers of the Presidents of the United States: John F. Kennedy, January 20, 1961 to December 31, 1961.* Washington, DC: Government Printing Office, 1962, pp. 1–3. Also, for a complete video of the inaugural speech, go to the website of the John F. Kennedy Presidential Library and Museum at www.jfklibrary.org/jfk/historic-speeches.aspx

General accounts of John Kennedy's presidency—See: James N. Giglio, *The Presidency of John F. Kennedy.* Lawrence: University Press of Kansas, 2006 (second edition); Robert Dallek, *An Unfinished Life: John F. Kennedy, 1917–1963.* Boston: Little, Brown, 2003; Barbara Leaming, *Jack Kennedy: The Education of a Statesman.* New York: W. W. Norton, 2006; Herbert Parmet, *JFK: The Presidency of John F. Kennedy.* New York: Penguin Books, 1984; Richard Reeves, *President Kennedy: Profile of Power.* New York: Simon and Schuster, 1993.

Bay of Pigs—For an overview of the Bay of Pigs incident, see: Howard Jones, *The Bay of Pigs.* New York: Oxford University Press, 2008; Peter Wyden, *Bay of Pigs: The Untold Story.* New York: Simon and Schuster, 1979; See also the Pulitzer Prize–winning journalist's account of this incident: Haynes Johnson, et al, *The Bay of Pigs: The Leaders' Story of Brigade 2506.* New York: W. W. Norton, 1964. For a ten-minute Universal Newsreel release reporting the aftermath of the failed invasion, go to the C-SPAN website, at www.c-spanvideo.org/program/Ba.

Cuban Missile Crisis—For a firsthand account of the Cuban Missile Crisis, see: Robert F. Kennedy, *Thirteen Days: A Memoir of the Cuban Missile Crisis.* New York: W. W. Norton, 1969. For a thorough discussion of the incident, see: Graham Allison, and Philip Zelikow, *Essence of Decision: Explaining the Cuban Missile Crisis.* New York: Longman, 1999. See also: Michael Dobbs, *One Minute to Midnight: Kennedy, Khrushchev, and Castro on the Brink of Nuclear War.* New York: Alfred A. Knopf, 2008; Ernest R. May, and Philip D. Zelikow, *The Kennedy Tapes: Inside the White*

House During the Cuban Missile Crisis. Cambridge, MA: Belknap Press of Harvard University, 1997; Max Frankel, *High Noon in the Cold War: Kennedy, Khrushchev, and the Cuban Missile Crisis.* New York: Ballantine Books, 2004. For a ten-minute Universal Newsreel release report on this crisis, go to the C-SPAN website, at www.c-spanvideo.org/program/301730-1.

Space race—For a short summary of the space race between the Soviet Union and the United States, go to the History Channel's website, at www.history.com/topics /space-race. See also: Von Hardesty, and Gene Eisman, *Epic Rivalry: The Inside Story of the Soviet and American Space Race.* Washington, DC: National Geographic, 2007; Matthew Brzezinski, *Red Moon Rising: Sputnik and the Hidden Rivalries That Ignited the Space Race.* New York: Times Books, 2007.

Space race speech at Rice University—See: *Public Papers of the Presidents of the United States: John F. Kennedy, January 1, 1962 to December 31, 1962.* Washington, DC: Government Printing Office, 1963, pp. 668–671. For a complete video of the speech, go to http://er.jsc.nasa.gov/seh/ricetalk.htm.

Berlin speech—See: *Public Papers of the Presidents of the United States: John F. Kennedy, January 1, 1962 to December 31, 1962.* Washington, DC: Government Printing Office, 1963, pp. 524–525. For newsreel footage of JFK's trip to Berlin in June 1963, go to www.c-spanvideo.org/program/153127-1.

Brown v. Board of Education—For an overview of this decision, see: Richard Kluger, *Simple Justice: The History of* Brown v. Board of Education *and Black America's Struggle for Equality.* New York: Vintage Books, 1977; James T. Patterson, *Brown v. Board of Education: A Civil Rights Milestone and Its Troubled Legacy.* New York: Oxford University Press, 2001.

Civil rights movement—For an account of civil rights activities during the Kennedy years, see: Juan Williams, *Eyes on the Prize: America's Civil Rights Years, 1954–1965.* New York: Viking, 1987; Taylor Branch, *Pillar of Fire: America in the King Years, 1963–1965.* New York: Simon and Schuster, 1998 (the second work in the trilogy by this author).

White House tour—This tour was broadcasted on all three television networks (ABC, CBS, and NBC). The complete broadcast can be found at www.youtube.com /watch?v=CbFt4h3Dkkw. See also: Perry Wolff, *A Tour of the White House with Mrs. John F. Kennedy.* Garden City, NY: Doubleday, 1962.

JFK's charisma—Numerous works have attempted to analyze John Kennedy's style. See: John Hellmann, *The Kennedy Obsession: The American Myth of JFK.* New York: Columbia University Press, 1997; Henry Fairlie, *The Kennedy Promise: The Politics of*

Expectation. Garden City, NY: Doubleday, 1973; David M. Lubin, *Shooting Kennedy: JFK and the Culture of Images*. Berkeley: University of California Press, 2003; Thomas Brown, *JFK: History of an Image*. Bloomington: Indiana University Press, 1988; John Goodman, *The Kennedy Mystique: Creating Camelot*. Washington, DC: National Geographic, 2006; Kitty Kelley, *Capturing Camelot: Stanley Tretick's Iconic Images of the Kennedys*. New York: Thomas Dunne Books, 2012; William Manchester, *One Brief Shining Moment*. Boston: Little, Brown, 1983; Richard Reeves, *Portrait of Camelot: A Thousand Days in the Kennedy White House*. New York: Abrams, 2010; Mark Shaw, *The John F. Kennedys: A Family Album*. New York: Rizzoli International Productions, 1966.

The trip to Dallas—See: William Manchester, *The Death of a President: November 20–November 25*. New York: Harper and Row, 1967; Vincent Bugliosi, *Reclaiming History: The Assassination of President John F. Kennedy*. New York: W. W. Norton, 2007,———. *Four Days in November: The Assassination of President John F. Kennedy*. New York: W. W. Norton, 2007; Gerald Blaine, *The Kennedy Detail: JFK's Secret Service Agents Break Their Silence*. New York: Gallery Books, 2010; Clint Hill, and Lisa McCubbin, *Mrs. Kennedy and Me*. New York: Gallery Books, 2012.

PART TWO: THE ASSASSINATION

Public announcement of parade route—The motorcade route, touring from Main to Houston to Elm and then onto the Stemmons Freeway, was revealed to the public by the two Dallas newspapers on November 19, 1963. See: United States. *Hearings Before the President's Commission on the Assassination of President John F. Kennedy*, 26 vols. Washington, DC: Government Printing Office, 1965. Vol. 22, Commission Exhibits 1362 and 1363.

Newspaper coverage—A very large-size publication was issued that reprinted, in newspaper format, the stories and title pages from the two Dallas papers for the events surrounding the assassination during the following two weeks. A smaller magazine-format version of this edition was also issued. See: *The Assassination Story: Newspaper Clippings from the Two Dallas Dailies*; The Dallas Morning News, *Nov. 23–Dec. 11, 1963;* The Dallas Times Herald, *Nov. 22–Dec. 10, 1963.*

Previous assassinations and attempts—For an overview on political assassinations in the United States, see: James W. Clarke, *American Assassins: The Darker Side of Politics*. Princeton, NJ: Princeton University Press, 1982; James McKinley, *Assassination in America*. New York: Harper and Row, 1977.

Oswald's life—There are numerous accounts of Oswald's life. For a primary source, firsthand account by his brother, see: Robert L. Oswald, Myrick Land, and Barbara

Land, *Lee: A Portrait of Lee Harvey Oswald*. New York: Coward-McCann, 1967. For an account by a journalist who knew Lee and Marina Oswald, see: Priscilla Johnson McMillan, *Marina and Lee*. New York: Harper and Row, 1977.

Oswald's rifle—An entire book has been published regarding the history of the purchase and use of the Mannlicher-Carcano rifle by Oswald. See: Henry S. Bloomgarden, *The Gun: A "Biography" of the Gun that Killed John F. Kennedy*. New York: Grossman, 1975.

Oswald's assassination attempt on General Edwin Walker—In its conclusion that Lee Harvey Oswald fired the shot that almost killed General Walker, the Warren Commission, evaluated the following evidence: (1) a note that Oswald left for his wife on the evening of the shooting, (2) photographs found among Oswald's possessions after the assassination of President Kennedy, (3) firearm identification of the bullet found in Walker's home, and (4) admissions and other statements made to Marina Oswald by Oswald concerning the shooting. See: *Report of the President's Commission on the Assassination of President John F. Kennedy*. Washington, DC: Government Printing Office, 1964, 183-187.

Oswald in New Orleans—In August 1963 in New Orleans, Oswald participated in one television and two radio appearances. The August 1963 interview on WDSU-TV can be found at www.youtube.com/watch?v=wYcylHB7Z9k. Numerous phonographic recordings of the radio appearance were commercially released, such as: *Oswald: Self-Portrait in Red*. Information Council of the Americas (Eyewitness Records), 1967. One of the principal participants in this radio debate also wrote a book on the assassination: Dr. Carlos Bringuier, *Red Friday: Nov. 22nd, 1963*. Chicago: C. Hallberg, 1969.

Oswald's relationship with Marina—For a detailed discussion of the relationship between Lee and Marina Oswald, see: McMillan, *Marina and Lee*. See also the Warren Commission testimony of Ruth Paine, who let Marina live with her in Dallas, and the testimony of Marina herself: Ruth Paine testimony (WC), vol. 3, pp. 430–525; vol. 9, pp. 1–139, 331–425; and vol. 11, pp. 153–155, 389–398; Marina Oswald's testimony, WC, vol. 1, pp. 1–126; vol. 5, pp. 387–408, 410–420, and 588–597; and vol. 11, pp. 275–301.

Oswald's threats to the FBI—See the testimony of James Patrick Hosty Jr., WC, vol. 4, pp. 440–476. See also: James P. Hosty Jr., *Assignment: Oswald*. New York: Arcade / Little, Brown, 1996. Hosty's papers are in the National Archives.

Oswald's life on the days leading up to the assassination See: Bugliosi, *Reclaiming History—Four Days in November*; Gerald L. Posner, *Case Closed: Lee Harvey Oswald and the Assassination of JFK*. New York: Random House, 1993; Thomas Mallon, *Mrs. Paine's Garage and the Murder of John F. Kennedy*. New York: Pantheon Books, 2002.

Oswald's November 21 planning— It is likely that by 10:00 a.m. on Thursday, November 21, Oswald had already decided to assassinate President Kennedy the next day. Between eight and ten o'clock in the morning on the twenty-first, Oswald asked Book Depository coworker Buell Wesley Frazier, "Could I get a ride home with you this afternoon?" When Frazier asked why, Oswald replied, "I am going home to get some curtain rods." Frazier agreed to drive Oswald that afternoon to Mrs. Paine's house, where Oswald had hidden his rifle. For details, see WC, vol. 2, p. 222.

Leaving the wedding ring and money behind— See the testimony of Marina Oswald, WC, vol. 1, p. 1; vol. 5. pp. 387, 410, 588; vol. 9, p. 275.

Oswald's curtain rods comment— See the testimony of Buell Wesley Frazier, WC, vol. 2, pp. 226–227 and pp. 210–245; vol. 7, p. 531.

Morning in Fort Worth, JFK and Jackie's conversation— See: Manchester, *The Death of the President; November 20–November 25, 1963*, p. 221.

The Secret Service's dislike of open car— See the testimony of Secret Service agent Roy Kellerman about bubbletop, WC, vol. 2, pp. 66–67 and pp. 61–112.

"There are no faint hearts in Fort Worth"— This outdoor address delivered to crowds in front of the Hotel Texas was given the morning of November 22. See: *Public Papers of the Presidents of the United States: John F. Kennedy, January 1, 1963 to November 22, 1963*. Washington, DC: Government Printing Office, 1964, p. 887. For the complete audio of this address, go to the JFK Fort Worth Tribute website, at www.jfktribute.com/videos. (There is also the complete video of the breakfast address to the Chamber of Congress.)

From Love Field to Dealey Plaza— For a firsthand account by Governor Connally's wife, who traveled in the presidential limousine from the time of the arrival at Love Field, see: Nellie Connally and Mickey Herskovitz, *From Love Field: Our Final Hours with President John F. Kennedy*. New York: Rugged Land, 2003. Also, for a DVD with rare video footage, see: *National Geographic: The Lost JFK Tapes — The Assassination*. 2010, excerpted at http://channel.nationalgeographic.com/channel/videos/jfks-assassination/.

Sun in Jackie's eyes— In journalist Theodore H. White's "Camelot" interview with Jacqueline Kennedy, in White's Library of Congress Papers, released in 1995, one year after her death.

Witnesses in closest proximity to Oswald— Three witnesses on the fifth floor of the Texas School Book Depository heard the shots coming from the sixth floor, with the sound of cartridge shells dropping on the floor and some cement falling from the ceiling. See the testimony of Bonnie Ray Williams, WC, vol. 3, pp. 161–184; Harold Norman, WC, vol. 3, pp. 186–198; and James "Junior" Jarman Jr., WC, vol. 3, pp. 198–211.

Filming of the assassination — See the testimony of Abraham Zapruder, WC, vol. 7, pp. 569–576. Today, there is always a "pool" camera covering the president's public movements. So any future attempt or attack on a president will always be filmed. This was not the case in November 1963. However, several still photographs and films were taken before, during, and after the assassination, of which Zapruder's was the most important and famous. There were many amateur and a few professional photographers and filmmakers in Dealey Plaza. Other important films include those taken from the other side of the Grassy Knoll by Orville Nix and Marie Muchmore. Also, important still photographs were taken by Phil Willis, James "Ike" Altgens, and Mary Moorman. For an illustration of where these individuals stood in Dealey Plaza, see: Josiah Thompson, *Six Seconds in Dallas: A Micro-study of the Kennedy Assassination.* New York: B. Geis / Random House, 1967, p. 12. For a comprehensive analysis of photographs taken that day, see: Richard B. Trask, *Pictures of the Pain: Photography and the Assassination of President Kennedy.* Danvers, MA: Yeoman, 1994. Copies of the Zapruder film were first "bootlegged" by Penn Jones Jr., publisher of the *Midlothian Mirror*, after Jim Garrison subpoenaed it as a part of his New Orleans investigation. The film was widely distributed and sold to the public. For black-and-white stills (along with Nix's and Muchmore's), see WC, vol. 18, pp. 1–95; and several color stills were published in *Life* magazine. Dan Rather of CBS News gave an audio narration of the film on TV in 1963. The first TV viewing of the film occurs on Geraldo Rivera's *Good Night America* on ABC in 1975. To view the first commercially released version of this film on VHS and later on DVD, see: *Image of an Assassination: A New Look at the Zapruder Film.* MPI Home Video, 1998. The comprehensive ninety-minute documentary, which also includes the original televised interview with Abraham Zapruder, can be seen at www.youtube.com/watch?v=vVafiaW4AdY.

The hearing of firecrackers — For examples of witnesses hearing firecrackers in Dealey Plaza, see the testimony of James Thomas Tague, WC, vol. 7, p. 553 (pp. 552–558); and the testimony of Secret Service agent Roy H. Kellerman, WC, vol. 2, p. 73 (pp. 61–112).

Jackie's reaction — See Theodore White's "Camelot" interview.

Trauma Room 1 — For a detailed account, see: Manchester, *The Death of a President*.

Oswald's movements at the Texas School Book Depository — See: Secret Service telephone comment/testimony of Roy S. Truly, superintendent of TSBD, WC, vol. 3, p. 212; vol. 7, pp. 380, 591; and many others.

First television announcement of assassination—Walter Cronkite interrupts the CBS daily broadcast of the soap opera *As the World Turns*. See the CBS website, at www.cbsnews.com/2100-500202_162-584646.html, and comprehensive coverage can be found on YouTube in ten parts. For the complete coverage, beginning with the first interruption, see: www.youtube.com/watch?v=qtXfZso-Bno and also an additional two hours of uninterrupted coverage at www.youtube.com/watch?v=t_Ry9-bpixM.

Accounts of how the news was reported—See: Newseum, Cathy Trost, and Susan Bennett, *President Kennedy Has Been Shot: Experience the Moment-to-Moment Account of the Four Days that Changed America*. Naperville, IL: Sourcebooks Mediafusion, 2003; Laura Hlavach, and Darwin Payne, eds., *Reporting the Kennedy Assassination: Journalists Who Were There Recall Their Experiences*. Dallas: Three Forks, 1996; John B. Mayo Jr., *Bulletin from Dallas: The President Is Dead; The Story of John F. Kennedy's Assassination as Covered by Radio and TV*. New York: Exposition, 1967; Robert B. Semple Jr., ed., *Four Days in November: The Original Coverage of the John F. Kennedy Assassination by the Staff of the* New York Times. New York: St. Martin's Press, 2003; Barbie Zelizer, *Covering the Body: The Kennedy Assassination, the Media, and the Shaping of Collective Memory*. Chicago: University of Chicago Press, 1992.

"Oh, no"—See the testimony of Jacqueline Kennedy, WC, vol. 5, pp. 180. (pp. 178–181).

Oswald's movements—Oswald's travels, including his bus and taxi rides, were reported by numerous witnesses to the Warren Commission.

"I want to be with him"—See Theodore White's "Camelot" interview.

The fight at Parkland Hospital for control of JFK's corpse—See: Manchester, *The Death of a President*.

Shooting of Officer Tippit; "poor dumb cop" comment by Oswald—See the testimony of William W. Scoggins, WC, vol. 2, p. 327 (pp. 322-340). The Warren Commission identified at least twelve people who witnessed the incident or aftermath.

LBJ takes oath—A firsthand diary account of the swearing-in was prepared by Marie Fehmer, President Johnson's secretary. Also, to see all the photographs taken by Cecil Stoughton on Air Force One, go to the "November 22, 1963 and Beyond" web page of the Lyndon Baines Johnson Library and Museum, at www.lbjlib.utexas.edu/johnson/kennedy/Oath of Office/oathphotos.htm.

"[W]ipe the blood off"—See Theodore White's "Camelot" interview.

Oswald's arrest—See the testimony of M. N. McDonald, WC, vol. 3, pp. 295–305.

Relationship between RFK and LBJ—Tensions between Robert F. Kennedy and Lyndon B. Johnson began during the 1960 presidential campaign. For a thorough treatment of this subject, see: Jeff Shesol, *Mutual Contempt: Lyndon Johnson, Robert Kennedy, and the Feud that Defined a Decade*. New York: W. W. Norton, 1997.

Johnson's comment of "I will do my best"—See: *Public Papers of the Presidents of the United States: Lyndon B. Johnson, November 22, 1963 to June 30, 1964*, 2 vols. Washington, DC: Government Printing Office, 1965, 1:1. For an audio recording of the president's remarks, as well as his handwritten notes on his statement, go to the Lyndon Baines Johnson Library and Museum website, at: www.lbjlib.utexas.edu /johnson/kennedy/Remarks%20at%20Andrews/remarks.htm.

The limousine flags—For the removal of the limousine flags, and for photographs of them, see the auction catalog in which they were offered for sale; John F. Kennedy, *The Robert L. White Collection*, Guernsey's. New York, NY. December 15, 16, 17, 2005, pages 248–249.

JFK autopsy—See: Manchester, *Death of a President*; Bugliosi, *Reclaiming History*.

Telling the children/Maud Shaw—Englishwoman Maud Shaw cared for the Kennedy children for seven years. For her account, see: Maud Shaw, *White House Nannie: My Years with Caroline and John Kennedy, Jr*. New York: New American Library, 1966.

Decision to bury at Arlington—For a discussion on the decision by Jackie to bury JFK at Arlington National Cemetery, and other information concerning the burial, go to the official website of the cemetery, at www.arlingtoncemetery.mil /visitorinformation/monumentmemorials/jfk.aspx.

Oswald's interrogation and public comments—For some of the comments made by Oswald from the time he left the Texas School Book Depository to when he was shot on Sunday, see: David Wallechinsky, and Irving Wallace, eds., *The People's Almanac #2*. New York: Morrow, 1978, pp. 47–52. For a video compilation of Oswald's utterances in the hallways of the Dallas police station, including responses to reporters' questions, go to: www.youtube.com/watch?v=4FDDuRSgzFk, and also: www.youtube .com/watch?v=tjphDSY5QJ4.

Excerpted Summary of Oswald's Words—In Texas Theatre—"Why should I hide my face? I haven't done anything to be ashamed of. . . . I want a lawyer. . . . I am not resisting arrest. . . . I didn't kill anybody. . . . I haven't shot anybody. . . . I protest this police brutality. . . . I fought back there, but I know I wasn't supposed to be carrying a gun. . . . What is this all about?" (Patrolman M. N. McDonald)

First lineup—"It isn't right to put me in line with these teenagers. . . . You know what you are doing, and you are trying to railroad me. . . . I want my lawyer."

Second lineup (shouting to reporters)—"I didn't shoot anyone. . . . I want to get in touch with a lawyer. . . . I never killed anybody."

Arraignment—"I insist upon my constitutional rights. . . . The way you are treating me, I might as well be in Russia."

Third lineup (yelling at reporters)—"I am only a patsy."

Press Conference—Asked about black eye: "A policeman hit me."

In interchange with reporters—"I really don't know what the situation is about. Nobody has told me anything except that I am accused of murdering a policeman. I know nothing more than that, and I do request someone to come forward to give me legal assistance."

When asked if he killed the president—"No. I have not been charged with that. In fact, nobody has said that to me yet. The first thing I heard about it was when the newspaper reporters in the hall asked me that question. . . . I did not do it. I did not do it. . . . I did not shoot anyone."

Sale of the Zapruder film—On November 25, 1963, *Life* magazine purchased the rights to the film plus royalties for $150,000, of which Abraham Zapruder donated $25,000 to Officer Tippit's widow. In 1975, the rights to the film, which was stored at the National Archives, were transferred back to the Zapruder family. In 1999, a special arbitration panel that had been established awarded the Zapruder family $16 million in compensation for the government's possession of the film. Later that year, the family donated all the copyrights of the film to the Sixth Floor Museum at Dealey Plaza in Dallas. For the timeline of the activities concerning this historical film, see the website of the museum at: www.jfk.org/go/collections/about/zapruder-film -chronology. For more on the Zapruder film, see: Richard B. Trask, *National Nightmare on Six Feet of Film: Mr. Zapruder's Home Movie and the Murder of President Kennedy.* Danvers, MA: Yeoman, 2005; Øyvind Vågnes, *Zaprudered: The Kennedy Assassination Film in the Visual Culture.* Austin: University of Texas Press, 2011.

Jackie's visit to Arlington Cemetery—For a comprehensive overview of the detailed planning of the funeral, see Billy C. Mossman, and B. C. Stark, *The Last Salute: Civil* *and Military Funerals, 1921–1969.* Washington, DC: Department of the Army, 1971, pp. 188–215.

Jackie/RFK private viewing of body—See: Manchester, *The Death of the President.*

Senator Mansfield's "took a ring" eulogy—There were also several other tributes in the U.S. Congress. See: U.S. Senate. *Memorial Addresses in the Congress of the United States and Tributes in Eulogy of John Fitzgerald Kennedy, Late a President of the United States.* Washington, DC: Government Printing Office, 1964.

Ruby shoots Oswald—For background material on the life of Jack Ruby, see: Melvin M. Belli, and Maurice C. Carroll, *Dallas Justice: The Real Story of Jack Ruby and His Trial.* New York: David McKay, 1964; Elmer Gertz, *Moment of Madness: The People vs. Jack Ruby.* Chicago: Follett, 1968; Garry Wills, and Ovid Demaris, *Jack Ruby: The Man Who Killed the Man Who Killed Kennedy.* New York: New American Library, 1968. For reminiscences by two strippers who worked for Jack Ruby, see: Diana Hunter, and Alice Anderson, *Jack Ruby's Girls.* Atlanta: Hallux, 1970.

Lying in state at Capitol—For picturesque color photographic coverage, see: Melville Bell Grosvenor, *The Last Full Measure: The World Pays Tribute to President Kennedy.* Washington, DC: National Geographic, 1964. (A specially issued reprint from the March 1964 issue of the magazine, pp. 307–355.) For an eight-minute Universal Newsreel release of coverage of the JFK funeral and burial, go to the C-SPAN website, at www.c-spanvideo.org/program/153113-1.

Presidential salute by John Jr.—See the account, "A Little Soldier's Salute," by Robert M. Andrews, a UPI correspondent, in: United Press International, ed., *Four Days: The Historical Record of the Death of President Kennedy.* New York: American Heritage, 1964, pp. 114-115.

John Jr.'s birthday party—See Theodore White's "Camelot" interview.

Oswald funeral—For an interview with Mike Cochran, an Associated Press reporter, that weaves the timelines of the three funerals of John F. Kennedy, Officer J. D. Tippit, and Lee Harvey Oswald that occured on Monday, November 25, 1963, see: "Nov. 22, Twenty-Five Years Later," *Dallas Morning News*, November 20, 1988, special pull-out section." Reprinted at: www.writespirit.net/wp-content/cache/supercache/www.writespirit.net/soulful-tributes/political-figures/president-kennedy/funeral-timeline-kennedy-john//. For photographs of the funeral, see: Marguerite Oswald, *Aftermath of an Execution: The Burial and Final Rites of Lee Harvey Oswald As Told by His Mother.* Dallas: Challenge, 1965; Robert J. Groden, *The Search for Lee Harvey Oswald: A Comprehensive Photographic Record.* New York: Penguin Studio Books, 1995.

EPILOGUE

Lyndon B. Johnson—For his November 27 address, see *Public Papers of the Presidents of the United States, Lyndon B. Johnson. 1963–1964*. Washington DC: Government Printing Office, 1965, Volume 1, pp. 8–10. For his statement on the Warren Commission, see p. 13. For his Executive Order 11130 creating the Warren Commission, see p. 14.

The Warren Commission—The members of the Warren Commission presented their one-volume report to President Johnson at the White House on Friday, September 24, 1964. That report was embargoed, and was not supposed to be released to the news media until Monday, September 27. Copies leaked out in advance, anyway. The twenty-six supporting volumes of testimony and exhibits collected by the Warren Commission were published and made available to the public in November 1964.

Letters of condolence—To read some of these letters, see: Ellen Fitzpatrick, ed., *Letters to Jackie: Condolences from a Grieving Nation*. New York: Ecco, 2010; Jay Mulvaney, and Paul De Angelis, *Dear Mrs. Kennedy: The World Shares Its Grief—Letters, November 1963*. New York: St. Martin's Press, 2010. On January 14, 1964, Jacqueline Kennedy appeared in a newsreel, which preceded the featured film in movie theaters throughout the country, to thank the nation for its outpouring of sympathy. For a video of her brief remarks, go to: www.youtube.com/watch?v=oJhAkD8LGwg.

For Jacqueline Kennedy's life after the assassination—See: Bill Adler, *The Eloquent Jacqueline Kennedy Onassis: A Portrait in Her Own Words*. New York: William Morrow, 2004; Christopher P. Andersen, *Jackie after Jack*. New York: William Morrow, 1998; Michael Beschloss, ed., *Jacqueline Kennedy: Historic Conversations on Life with John F. Kennedy*. New York: Hyperion, 2011; Bradford, *America's Queen: The Life of Jacqueline Kennedy Onassis*; Heymann, *A Woman Named Jackie*; William M. Kuhn, *Reading Jackie: Her Autobiography in Books*. New York: Nan A. Talese / Doubleday, 2010; Greg Lawrence, *Jackie as Editor: The Literary Life of Jacqueline Kennedy Onassis*. New York: Thomas Dunne Books, 2011.

Conspiracy Theories—For brief coverage of the history, chronology, and diversity of the conspiracy theories, see Peter Knight's books *The Kennedy Assassination* and *Conspiracy Culture: From Kennedy to The X-Files*. For the most comprehensive analysis of the theories, and for the most thorough arguments against them, see Vincent Bugliosi's *Reclaiming History*, and Gerald Posner's *Case Closed*.

FOR FURTHER READING

The bibliography of the Kennedy assassination is enormous. There are thousands of published books, magazines, pamphlets, and articles on the subject. No bibliography has ever listed them all. No person has read them all. No one ever will. In addition to these published sources, millions of pages of documents in government files and elsewhere pertain in some way to the history of the assassination of President Kennedy. Thus, anyone who wishes to read further on the subject must be selective.

History is more than a narrative of what happened at a particular moment in time — it is also the story of how events were reported to, and experienced by, the people who lived through them. John Kennedy died in 1963. It was a time before cable television and hundreds if not thousands of channels; before personal computers, laptops, tablets, and smartphones; before cell phones, digital cameras, and video; before CDs, DVDs, or MP3s; before e-mails and tweets. Today, in an instant, Americans can transmit or receive information, breaking news, images, or videos anywhere at anytime. In November 1963, it was impossible for one American to even leave a simple voice message on another one's telephone. And if you wanted to make or receive a call, you had to do it from your home or office, where the phone was connected to a wire attached to a wall — mobile phones did not exist.

Today, people can obtain news from almost a countless number and variety of sources. In the fall of 1963, the American people learned about events in a limited number of ways: from reading their local newspapers, listening to the radio, or watching small, black-and-white television screens that showed no more than four or five channels.

On November 22, 1963, the American people experienced the assassination of John F. Kennedy as a shared event. On the same day at the same time, an entire nation read the same stories, saw the same photographs, and watched the same images on television. For four days straight, the three national television news networks—CBS, NBC, and ABC—immersed the American people in a shared moment of national grief. For the first time in U.S. history, the medium of television unified a nation through its coverage of a historic event. Similarly, the great weekly picture magazines, *Life* and *Look*, published photos and stories seen by tens of millions of people.

It was a different time, historic not only for what happened but also for how the death of a president was reported and experienced. Once the story was over, people did not throw away their old newspapers and magazines. Instead, they preserved them as iconic family heirlooms, as time capsules for future generations. All over the nation, people put them away in basements, attics, and closets, where they can still be found today. There is no better way to learn how America experienced the assassination of President Kennedy and the days that followed than by going back to these original sources. As you turn the pages of these publications, reading the words and lingering on the photographs, and as you watch the old TV news broadcasts, now available on the web, you will travel back in time and imagine what it was like to be alive on November 22, 1963.

The first major book on the Kennedy assassination was the *Report of the President's Commission on the Assassination of President John F. Kennedy* (the "Warren Report"). Published in 1964 by the official U.S. government commission appointed by President Lyndon B. Johnson to investigate the Kennedy assassination, and chaired by Chief Justice Earl Warren, the report concluded, in my opinion correctly, that Lee Harvey Oswald killed President Kennedy, that he acted alone, and that there was no evidence that he was part of a conspiracy. The Warren Report inaugurated a deluge of books on the Kennedy assassination that has not subsided to this day.

The bibliography that follows lists most of the books that I consulted while researching *"The President Has Been Shot!"* Readers will enjoy two commemorative illustrated books published not long after the assassination, United Press International's *Four Days: The Historical Record of the Death of President Kennedy* and the Associated Press's *The Torch is Passed: The Associated Press Story of the Death of a President.*

For more on the sites connected to the assassination, including the Texas School Book Depository, and for a brief introduction to the story, see Conover Hunt's *Dealey Plaza National Historic Landmark Including the Sixth Floor Museum.*

The two best books in support of the true version of the assassination — that Lee Harvey Oswald killed the president — are Gerald Posner's *Case Closed: Lee Harvey Oswald and the Assassination of JFK* and Vincent Bugliosi's *Reclaiming History.* For readers deterred by the length of Bugliosi's book, I recommend his shorter account, *Four Days in November.* I certainly suggest reading Posner and Bugliosi before any of the conspiracy-oriented books on the events of November 22. For a brief and excellent introduction to the subject, on how it was reported, and for insightful commentary on the history and psychology of JFK conspiracy theories, see Peter Knight's *The Kennedy Assassination*. For an incisive analysis that places these theories within the larger context of the modern obsession with conspiracy interpretations of a number of twentieth-century events, see Knight's *Conspiracy Culture: From Kennedy to The X-Files*.

For a compelling narrative on the odd life of Lee Harvey Oswald, written by a woman who knew Oswald and his wife (and, strangely, John Kennedy too), see Priscilla Johnson McMillan's *Marina and Lee*.

For more on the life of JFK, see James N. Giglio's *The Presidency of John F. Kennedy*, and Robert Dallek's *An Unfinished Life: John F. Kennedy, 1917–1963*.

Thomas Mallon's *Mrs. Paine's Garage and the Murder of John F. Kennedy* remains one of my favorite books on the assassination. More than almost any work on the subject, it resurrects the emotions of that terrible day in Dallas, fifty years ago.

BIBLIOGRAPHY

GENERAL REFERENCES

Adler, Bill. *The Eloquent Jacqueline Kennedy Onassis: A Portrait in Her Own Words.* New York: William Morrow, 2004.

Allison, Graham, and Philip Zelikow. *Essence of Decision: Explaining the Cuban Missile Crisis.* New York: Longman, 1999.

Alsop, Stewart. *The Center: People and Power in Political Washington.* New York: Harper and Row, 1968.

Andersen, Christopher P. *Jackie after Jack.* New York: William Morrow, 1998.

Beschloss, Michael, ed. *Jacqueline Kennedy: Historic Conversations on Life with John F. Kennedy.* New York: Hyperion, 2011.

Bradford, Sarah. *America's Queen: The Life of Jacqueline Kennedy Onassis.* New York: Viking, 2000.

Branch, Taylor. *Pillar of Fire: America in the King Years, 1963–1965.* New York: Simon and Schuster, 1998.

Brzezinski, Matthew. *Red Moon Rising: Sputnik and the Hidden Rivalries that Ignited the Space Race.* New York: Times Books, 2007.

Brown, Thomas. *JFK: The History of an Image.* Bloomington: Indiana University Press, 1988.

Caro, Robert A. *The Passage of Power: The Years of Lyndon Johnson.* New York: Alfred A. Knopf, 2012.

Collier, Peter, and David Horowitz. *The Kennedys: An American Drama.* New York: Summit Books, 1984.

Dallek, Robert. *An Unfinished Life: John F. Kennedy, 1917–1963.* Boston: Little, Brown, 2003.

Davis, John H. *The Kennedys: Dynasty and Disaster, 1848–1983*. New York: McGraw-Hill, 1984.

Dobbs, Michael. *One Minute to Midnight: Kennedy, Khrushchev, and Castro on the Brink of Nuclear War*. New York: Alfred A. Knopf, 2008.

Donovan, Robert J. *PT 109: John F. Kennedy in World War II*. New York: McGraw-Hill, 1961.

Fairlie, Henry. *The Kennedy Promise: The Politics of Expectation*. Garden City, NY: Doubleday, 1973.

Frankel, Max. *High Noon in the Cold War: Kennedy, Khrushchev, and the Cuban Missile Crisis*. New York: Ballantine Books, 2004.

Garside, Anne, and Orlando Suero. *Camelot at Dawn: Jacqueline and John Kennedy in Georgetown, May 1954*. Baltimore: Johns Hopkins University Press, 2001.

Giglio, James N. *The Presidency of John F. Kennedy*. Lawrence: University Press of Kansas, 2006. Second edition.

Goodman, John. *The Kennedy Mystique: Creating Camelot*. Washington, DC: National Georgraphic, 2006.

Hamilton, Nigel. *JFK: Reckless Youth*. New York: Random House, 1992.

Hardesty, Von, and Gene Eisman. *Epic Rivalry: The Inside Story of the Soviet and American Space Race*. Washington, DC: National Geographic, 2007.

Hellmann, John. *The Kennedy Obsession: The American Myth of JFK*. New York: Columbia University Press, 1997.

Heymann, C. David. *A Woman Named Jackie*. Secaucus, NJ: Carol Communications, 1989.

Hill, Clint, and Lisa McCubbin. *Mrs. Kennedy and Me*. New York: Gallery Books, 2012.

Hosty, James P., Jr. *Assignment: Oswald*. New York: Arcade / Little, Brown, 1996.

Hunter, Diana, and Alice Anderson. *Jack Ruby's Girls*. Atlanta: Hallux, 1970.

Johnson, Haynes, et al. *The Bay of Pigs: The Leaders' Story of Brigade 2506*. New York: W. W. Norton, 1964.

Jones, Howard. *The Bay of Pigs*. New York: Oxford University Press, 2008.

Kelley, Kitty. *Capturing Camelot: Stanley Tretick's Iconic Images of the Kennedys*. New York: Thomas Dunne Books, 2012.

Kennedy, John F. *Public Papers of the Presidents of the United States: John F. Kennedy, 1961–1963*, 3 vols. Washington, DC: Government Printing Office, 1962–64.

Kennedy, Robert F. *Thirteen Days: A Memoir of the Cuban Missile Crisis*. New York: W. W. Norton, 1969.

Klein, Edward. *All Too Human: The Love Story of Jack and Jackie Kennedy*. New York: Pocket Books, 1996.

Kluger, Richard. *Simple Justice: The History of* Brown v. Board of Education *and Black America's Struggle for Equality*. New York: Vintage Books, 1977.

Kraus, Sidney, ed. *The Great Debates: Background, Perspective, Effects*. Bloomington: Indiana University Press, 1962.

Kuhn, William. *Reading Jackie: Her Autobiography in Books*. New York: Nan A. Talese / Doubleday, 2010.

Lawrence, Greg. *Jackie as Editor: The Literary Life of Jacqueline Kennedy Onassis*. New York: Thomas Dunne Books, 2011.

Leamer, Laurence. *The Kennedy Women: The Saga of an American Family*. New York: Villard Books, 1994.

Leaming, Barbara. *Jack Kennedy: The Education of a Statesman*. New York: W. W. Norton, 2006.

—— *Mrs. Kennedy: The Missing History of the Kennedy Years*. New York: Free Press, 2001.

Lubin, David M. *Shooting Kennedy: JFK and the Culture of Images*. Berkeley: University of California Press, 2003.

Manchester, William. *One Brief Shining Moment*. Boston: Little, Brown, 1983.

Matthews, Chris. *Jack Kennedy: Elusive Hero*. New York: Simon and Schuster, 2011.

—— *Kennedy & Nixon: The Rivalry that Shaped America*. New York: Simon and Schuster, 1996.

May, Ernest R., and Philip D. Zelikow. *The Kennedy Tapes: Inside the White House During the Cuban Missile Crisis*. Cambridge, MA: Belknap Press of Harvard University, 1997.

McKinley, James. *Assassination in America*. New York: Harper and Row, 1977.

Minow, Newton N., and Craig L. LaMay. *Inside the Presidential Debates: Their Improbable Past and Promising Future*. Chicago: University of Chicago Press, 2008.

Nasaw, David. *The Patriarch: The Remarkable Life and Turbulent Times of Joseph P. Kennedy*. New York: Penguin Press, 2012.

O'Donnell, Kenneth P., and David F. Powers, with Joe McCarthy. *"Johnny, We Hardly Knew Ye": Memories of John Fitzgerald Kennedy*. Boston: Little, Brown, 1972.

Oswald, Robert L., Myrick Land, and Barbara Land. *Lee: A Portrait of Lee Harvey Oswald*. New York: Coward-McCann, 1967.

Parmet, Herbert. *Jack: The Struggles of John F. Kennedy*. New York: Dial Press, 1980.

——— *JFK: The Presidency of John F. Kennedy*. New York: Penguin Books, 1984.

Patterson, James T. Brown v. Board of Education*: A Civil Rights Milestone and Its Troubled Legacy*. New York: Oxford University Press, 2001.

Perry, Barbara A. *Jacqueline Kennedy: First Lady of the New Frontier*. Lawrence: University Press of Kansas, 2004.

Piereson, James. *Camelot and the Cultural Revolution: How the Assassination of John F. Kennedy Shattered American Liberalism*. New York: Encounter Books, 2007.

Reeves, Richard. *Portrait of Camelot: A Thousand Days in the Kennedy White House*. New York: Abrams, 2010.

——— *President Kennedy: Profile of Power*. New York: Simon and Schuster, 1993.

Renehan, Edward J., Jr. *The Kennedys at War: 1937–1945*. New York: Doubleday, 2002.

Schieffer, Bob. *This Just In: What I Couldn't Tell You on TV*. New York: G. P. Putnam's Sons, 2003.

Schlesinger, Arthur M., Jr. *A Thousand Days: John F. Kennedy in the White House*. Boston: Houghton Mifflin, 1965.

——. *Kennedy or Nixon: Does It Make Any Difference?* New York: Macmillan, 1960.

Shaw, Mark. *The John F. Kennedys: A Family Album*. New York: Rizzoli, 2000. Revised edition.

Shaw, Maud. *White House Nannie: My Years with Caroline and John Kennedy, Jr.* New York: New American Library, 1966.

Shesol, Jeff. *Mutual Contempt: Lyndon Johnson, Robert Kennedy, and the Feud that Defined an Era*. New York: W. W. Norton, 1997.

Smith, Sally Bedell. *Grace and Power: The Private World of the Kennedy White House*. New York: Random House, 2004.

Whalen, Richard J. *The Founding Father: The Story of Joseph P. Kennedy*. New York: New American Library, 1964.

Wicker, Tom. *JFK and LBJ: The Influence of Personality upon Politics*. New York: Morrow, 1968.

——. *Kennedy Without Tears: The Man Beneath the Myth*. New York: Morrow, 1964.

Widmer, Ted, ed. *Listening In: The Secret White House Recordings of John F. Kennedy*. New York: Hyperion, 2012.

Williams, Juan. *Eyes on the Prize: America's Civil Rights Years, 1954–1965*. New York: Viking Press, 1987.

Wolff, Perry. *A Tour of the White House with Mrs. John F. Kennedy*. Garden City, NY: Doubleday, 1962.

Wyden, Peter. *Bay of Pigs: The Untold Story*. New York: Simon and Schuster, 1979.

Youngblood, Rufus W. *20 Years in the Secret Service: My Life with Five Presidents*. New York: Simon and Schuster, 1973.

THE ASSASSINATION

Associated Press. *The Torch Is Passed: The Associated Press Story of the Death of a President.* New York: Associated Press, 1963.

Belli, Melvin M., and Maurice C. Carroll. *Dallas Justice: The Real Story of Jack Ruby and His Trial.* New York: David McKay, 1964.

Bishop, Jim. *The Day Kennedy Was Shot.* New York: Funk and Wagnalls, 1968.

Blaine, Gerald. *The Kennedy Detail: JFK's Secret Service Agents Break Their Silence.* New York: Gallery Books, 2010.

Bloomgarden, Henry S. *The Gun: A "Biography" of the Gun that Killed John F. Kennedy.* New York: Grossman, 1975.

Bringuier, Dr. Carlos. *Red Friday: Nov. 22nd, 1963.* Chicago: C. Hallberg, 1969.

Bugliosi, Vincent. *Four Days in November: The Assassination of President John F. Kennedy.* New York: W. W. Norton, 2007.

────── *Reclaiming History: The Assassination of President John F. Kennedy.* New York: W. W. Norton & Company, 2007.

Callahan, Bob. *Who Shot JFK?: A Guide to the Major Conspiracy Theories.* New York: Simon and Schuster, 1993.

Clarke, James W. *American Assassins: The Darker Side of Politics.* Princeton, NJ: Princeton University Press, 1982.

Connally, Nellie, and Mickey Herskowitz. *From Love Field: Our Final Hours with President John F. Kennedy.* New York: Rugged Land, 2003.

Curry, Jesse E. *Retired Dallas Police Chief Jesse Curry Reveals His Personal JFK Assassination File.* Dallas: American Poster and Printing, 1969.

Eddowes, Michael. *The Oswald File.* New York: C. N. Potter / Crown, 1977.

Fitzpatrick, Ellen, ed. *Letters to Jackie: Condolences from a Grieving Nation.* New York: Ecco, 2010.

Ford, Gerald R., and John R. Stiles. *Portrait of the Assassin.* New York: Simon and Schuster, 1965.

Gertz, Elmer. *Moment of Madness: The People vs. Jack Ruby.* Chicago: Follett, 1968.

Gillon, Steven M. *The Kennedy Assassination—24 Hours After: Lyndon B. Johnson's Pivotal First Day as President.* New York: Basic Books, 2009.

Grosvenor, Melville Bell. *The Last Full Measure: The World Pays Tribute to President Kennedy.* Washington, DC: National Geographic, 1964.

Hampton, Wilborn. *Kennedy Assassinated! The World Mourns: A Reporter's Story.* Cambridge, MA: Candlewick Press, 1997.

Harris, Patricia Howard. *An Austin Scrapbook of John F. Kennedy.* Austin: Pemberton Press, 1964.

Hlavach, Laura, and Darwin Payne, eds. *Reporting the Kennedy Assassination: Journalists Who Were There Recall Their Experiences.* Dallas: Three Forks Press, 1996.

Holland, Max. *The Kennedy Assassination Tapes.* New York: Alfred A. Knopf / Random House, 2004.

Hunt, Conover. *Dealey Plaza National Historic Landmark Including the Sixth Floor Museum.* Dallas: The Sixth Floor Museum, 1997.

Knight, Peter. *The Kennedy Assassination.* Jackson: University Press of Mississippi, 2007.

Lattimer, John K. *Kennedy and Lincoln: Medical and Ballistic Comparisons of Their Assassinations.* New York: Harcourt Brace Jovanovich, 1980.

Lewis, Richard Warren. *The Scavengers and Critics of the Warren Report: The Endless Paradox. Based on an Investigation by Lawrence Schiller.* New York: Delacorte Press, 1967.

Loken, John. *Oswald's Trigger Films: The Manchurian Candidate, We Were Strangers, Suddenly.* Ann Arbor: Falcon Books, 2000.

Mailer, Norman. *Oswald's Tale: An American Mystery.* New York: Random House, 1995.

Mallon, Thomas. *Mrs. Paine's Garage and the Murder of John F. Kennedy.* New York: Pantheon Books, 2002.

Manchester, William. *The Death of a President: November 20–November 25.* New York: Harper and Row, 1967.

Mayo, John B., Jr. *Bulletin from Dallas: The President Is Dead; The Story of John F. Kennedy's Assassination as Covered by Radio and TV*. New York: Exposition Press, 1967.

McMillan, Priscilla Johnson. *Marina and Lee*. New York: Harper and Row, 1977.

Mossman, Billy C., and B. C. Stark. *The Last Salute: Civil and Military Funerals, 1921–1969*. Washington, DC: Department of the Army, 1971.

Mulvaney, Jay, and Paul De Angelis. *Dear Mrs. Kennedy: The World Shares Its Grief—Letters, November 1963*. New York: St. Martin's Press, 2010.

Newseum, Cathy Trost, and Susan Bennett. *President Kennedy Has Been Shot: Experience the Moment-to-Moment Account of the Four Days that Changed America*. Naperville, IL: Sourcebooks Mediafusion, 2003.

NBC News. *Seventy Hours and Thirty Minutes, as Broadcast on the NBC Television Network by NBC News*. New York: Random House, 1966.

Oswald, Marguerite. *Aftermath of an Execution: The Burial and Final Rites of Lee Harvey Oswald As Told by His Mother*. Dallas: Challenge, 1965.

Posner, Gerald. *Case Closed: Lee Harvey Oswald and the Assassination of JFK*. New York: Random House, 1993.

Semple, Robert B., Jr., ed. *Four Days in November: The Original Coverage of the John F. Kennedy Assassination by the Staff of the* New York Times. New York: St. Martin's Press, 2003.

Sparrow, John. *After the Assassination: A Positive Appraisal of the Warren Report*. New York: Chilmark Press, 1967.

Sturdivan, Larry M. *The JFK Myths: A Scientific Investigation of the Kennedy Assassination*. St. Paul, MN: Paragon House, 2005.

Trask, Richard B. *National Nightmare on Six Feet of Film: Mr. Zapruder's Home Movie and the Murder of President Kennedy*. Danvers, MA: Yeoman Press, 2005.

——. *Pictures of the Pain: Photography and the Assassination of President Kennedy*. Danvers, MA: Yeoman Press, 1994.

——. *That Day in Dallas: Three Photographers Capture on Film the Day President Kennedy Died*. Danvers, MA: Yeoman Press, 1998.

United Press International. *Four Days: The Historical Record of the Assassination of President Kennedy*. New York: American Heritage, 1964.

U.S. Senate. *Memorial Addresses in the Congress of the United States and Tributes in Eulogy of John Fitzgerald Kennedy, Late a President of the United States*. Washington, DC: Government Printing Office, 1964.

Vâgnes, Øyvind. *Zaprudered: The Kennedy Assassination Film in the Visual Culture*. Austin: University of Texas Press, 2011.

Wallechinsky, David, and Irving Wallace, eds. *The People's Almanac #2*. New York: Morrow, 1978.

Walsh, William G. *Children Write about John F. Kennedy*. Brownsville, TX: Springman-King, 1964.

Warren Report. *Report of the President's Commission on the Assassination of President John F. Kennedy*. Washington, DC: Government Printing Office, 26 vols., 1964.

White, Stephen. *Should We Now Believe the Warren Report?* New York: Macmillan, 1968.

Wilber, Charles G. *Medicolegal Investigation of the President John F. Kennedy Murder*. Springfield, IL: C. C. Thomas, 1978.

Wills, Garry, and Ovid Demaris. *Jack Ruby: The Man Who Killed the Man Who Killed Kennedy*. New York: New American Library, 1968.

Wolfenstein, Martha, and Gilbert Kliman, eds. *Children and the Death of a President: Multi-disciplinary Studies*. Garden City, NY: Doubleday, 1965.

Zelizer, Barbie. *Covering the Body: The Kennedy Assassination, the Media, and the Shaping of Collective Memory*. Chicago: University of Chicago Press, 1992.

CONSPIRACY LITERATURE

These are some of the principal and most influential books that have advanced one or more of the various conspiracy theories of the assassination of President Kennedy. Although I have consulted them, their inclusion in this bibliography does not mean that I endorse any of them or support any of their theories.

Baker, Judyth Vary. *Me & Lee: How I Came to Know, Love and Lose Lee Harvey Oswald*. Walterville, OR: Trine Day. 2010.

Bonner, Judy Whitson. *Investigation of a Homicide: The Murder of John F. Kennedy*. Anderson, SC: Droke House / Grosset and Dunlap, 1969.

Douglass, James W. *JFK and the Unspeakable: Why He Died and Why It Matters*. Maryknoll, NY: Orbis Books, 2008.

Epstein, Edward J. *Inquest: The Warren Commission and the Establishment of Truth*. New York: Viking, 1966.

Fenster, Mark. *Conspiracy Theories: Secrecy and Power in American Culture*. Minneapolis: University of Minnesota Press, 1999.

Fonzi, Gaeton. *The Last Investigation*. New York: Thunder's Mouth, 1993.

Groden, Robert J. *The Killing of a President: The Complete Photographic Record of the JFK Assassination, the Conspiracy and the Cover-Up*. New York: Viking Studio Books, 1993.

———. *The Search for Lee Harvey Oswald: The Comprehensive Photographic Record*. New York: Penguin Studio Books, 1995.

Kaiser, David E. *The Road to Dallas: The Assassination of JFK*. Cambridge, MA: Belknap Press of Harvard University, 2008.

Kelin, John. *Praise from a Future Generation: The Assassination of John F. Kennedy and the First Generation Critics of the Warren Report*. San Antonio: Wings, 2007.

Kurtz, Michael L. *Crime of the Century: The Kennedy Assassination from a Historian's Perspective*. Knoxville: University of Tennessee Press, 1982.

———. *The JFK Assassination Debates: Lone Gunman versus Conspiracy*. Lawrence: University Press of Kansas, 2006.

Lane, Mark. *Rush to Judgment: A Critique of the Warren Commission's Inquiry into the Murders of President John F. Kennedy, Officer J. D. Tippit and Lee Harvey Oswald*. New York: Holt, Rinehart and Winston, 1966.

———. *Last Word: My Indictment of the CIA in the Murder of JFK*. New York: Skyhorse, 2011.

Lifton, David S. *Best Evidence: Disguise and Deception in the Assassination of John F. Kennedy*. New York: Macmillan, 1980.

Marrs, Jim. *Crossfire: The Plot That Killed Kennedy*. New York: Carroll and Graf, 1989.

McKnight, Gerald D. *Breach of Trust: How the Warren Commission Failed the Nation and Why*. Lawrence: University Press of Kansas, 2005.

Meagher, Sylvia. *Accessories After the Fact: The Warren Commission, the Authorities, and the Report*. Indianapolis: Bobbs-Merrill, 1967.

Newman, John. *Oswald and the CIA: The Documented Truth about the Unknown Relationship between the U.S. Government and the Alleged Killer of JFK*. New York: Skyhorse, 2008.

Russo, Gus. *Live by the Sword: The Secret War Against Castro and the Death of JFK*. Baltimore: Bancroft / National Book Network, 1998.

Russo, Gus, and Stephen Molton. *Brothers in Arms: The Kennedys, the Castros, and the Politics of Murder*. New York: Bloomsbury, 2008.

Sauvage, Leo. *The Oswald Affair: An Examination of the Contradictions and Omissions of the Warren Report*. Cleveland: World Publishing, 1966.

Schotz, Martin. *History Will Not Absolve Us: Orwellian Control, Public Denial, and the Murder of President Kennedy*. Kurtz, Olmer and Delucia, 1996.

Thompson, Josiah. *Six Seconds in Dallas: A Micro-study of the Kennedy Assassination*. New York: B. Geis / Random House, 1967.

Weisberg, Harold. *Oswald in New Orleans: Case for Conspiracy with the CIA*. Ipswich, MA: Mary Ferrell Foundation, 2006.

Wrone, David R. *The Zapruder Film: Reframing JFK's Assassination*. Lawrence: University of Kansas Press, 2003.

PHOTO CREDITS

MAPS

Pages 66–67: Gene Thorp/Cartographic Concepts

Page 113: Gene Thorp/Cartographic Concepts

Page 151: Gene Thorp/Cartographic Concepts

Pages 214–215, 216–217, 218–219, 220–221: © Graphics by John Grimwade

PHOTOS

Jacket front (top): Tom Dillard, *Dallas Morning News*/Corbis

Jacket front (bottom): Cecil Stoughton, White House Photographs/John F. Kennedy Presidential Library and Museum, Boston

Jacket back (hardcover): Dallas Municpal Archives/Portal to Texas History

Back cover (Scholastic Special Edition): Bettmann/Corbis

Case cover stamp (hardcover): National Archives

Jacket front flap: Bettmann /Corbis

Jacket back flap and page 274: Lisa Nipp

Page i: Carl Mydans/Time & Life Pictures/Getty Images

Pages ii–iii: Dallas Municipal Archives/Portal to Texas History

Pages iv–v: Dallas Municipal Archives/Portal to Texas History

Pages vi–vii (view from the sniper's nest): R.W. "Rusty" Livingston Collection /The Sixth Floor Museum at Dealey Plaza

Page viii: © 2000 Mark Shaw/mptvimages.com

Page x: AP Images

Pages xii–xiii: Bettmann/Corbis

Pages 2–3: Richard Sears/John F. Kennedy Presidential Library and Museum, Boston

Page 4: Naval Historical Center

Page 6: Toni Frissell Collection, Library of Congress

Pages 12–13: AP Images

Pages 18–19: Bettmann/Corbis

Page 21: AP Images

Page 25: Popperfoto/Getty Images

Page 26: Leslie Gilbert Illingworth/*Daily Mail*

Page 28: NASA

Page 30: Robert Knudsen White House Photographs/John F. Kennedy Presidential Library and Museum, Boston

Page 32: Apic/Getty Images

Pages 36–37: Bill Hudson/AP Images

Page 38: Cecil Stoughton, White House Photographs/John F. Kennedy Presidential Library and Museum, Boston

Pages 40–41: AP Images

Page 44: Cecil Stoughton, White House Photographs/John F. Kennedy Presidential Library and Museum, Boston

Pages 46–47: Corbis

Page 53: National Archives

Page 55: Corbis Images

Page 57: National Archives

Page 59: Corbis

Page 63: Dallas Municipal Archives/Portal to Texas History

Pages 64–65: Squire Haskins Photography, Inc. Collection, Special Collections, The University of Texas at Arlington Library

Page 69: Dallas Municipal Archives/The Portal to Texas History

Page 71: William Allen, photographer, *Dallas Times Herald* Collection/The Sixth Floor Museum at Dealey Plaza

Pages 74–75: AP Images

Page 76: The National Archives

Page 80: Courtesy *The Dallas Morning News*

Page 81: Cecil Stoughton, White House Photographs/John F. Kennedy Presidential Library and Museum, Boston

Page 82: Cecil Stoughton, White House Photographs/John F. Kennedy Presidential Library and Museum, Boston

Page 86: Cecil Stoughton White House Photographs/John F. Kennedy Presidential Library and Museum, Boston

Page 87: Art Rickerby/Time & Life Pictures/Getty Images

Page 89: Tom C. Dillard Collection, *The Dallas Morning News*/The Sixth Floor Museum at Dealey Plaza

Pages 90–91: Tom C. Dillard Collection, *The Dallas Morning News*/The Sixth Floor Museum at Dealey Plaza

Page 94: AP Images

Page 97: Darryl Heikes, photographer, *Dallas Times Herald* Collection/The Sixth Floor Museum at Dealey Plaza

Page 101: National Archives

Page 104: National Archives

Page 115: Tom C. Dillard Collection, *The Dallas Morning News*/The Sixth Floor Museum at Dealey Plaza

Page 116 (bottom): AP Image

Page 116 (top and center): Zapruder Film © 1967 (renewed 1995) The Sixth Floor Museum at Dealey Plaza

Page 118 (all): Zapruder Film © 1967 (renewed 1995) The Sixth Floor Museum at Dealey Plaza

Page 120 (top): Zapruder Film © 1967 (renewed 1995) The Sixth Floor Museum at Dealey Plaza

Page 120 (center and bottom): AP Images

Page 123: Al Volkland, photographer, *Dallas Times Herald* Collection/The Sixth Floor Museum at Dealey Plaza

Page 124: Dallas Municipal Archives/Portal to Texas History

Page 131: Bettmann/Corbis

Page 132: Cecil Stoughton, White House photographs/John Fitzgerald Kennedy Library and Museum, Boston

Page 135: CBS Photo Archive/Getty Images

Pages 136–137: Carl Mydans/Time & Life Pictures/Getty Images

Page 138: Library of Congress

Page 139: Andy Hanson © 2008, the Estate of Andrew A. Hanson, courtesy Photographic Archives Lab & Gallery, Dallas

Page 141: Darryl Heikes, photographer, *Dallas Times Herald* Collection/The Sixth Floor Museum at Dealey Plaza

Page 143: Cecil Stoughton, White House Photographs/John F. Kennedy Presidential Library and Museum, Boston

Pages 148–149: Cecil Stoughton, White House/John F. Kennedy Presidential Library and Museum, Boston

Pages 152–153: Archive Photos/Getty Images

Page 156: Wally McNamee/Corbis

Page 157: Bettmann/Corbis

Page 159: AP Images

Page 160: Robert Phillips/Time & Life Pictures/Getty Images

Page 162: Corbis

Page 165: Bettmann/Corbis

Page 167: *Dallas Times Herald* Collection/The Sixth Floor Museum at Dealey Plaza

Page 168: Corbis

Page 169: Tom Dillard/*The Dallas Morning News*/Corbis

Page 171: Bettmann/Corbis

Page 173: Bettmann/Corbis

Pages 174–175: Bettmann/Corbis

Page 176: Bettmann/Corbis

Pages 178–179: Bettmann/Corbis

Page 181: Bettmann/Corbis

Page 182: Bettmann/Corbis

Page 183: Corbis

Page 185: © Bob Jackson

Page 186: AP Images

Page 189: AP Images

Pages 190–191: Oliver F. Atkins photograph collection/Special Collections & Archives/George Mason University Libraries

Page 192: Gamma-Keystone/Getty Images

Page 194: Bettmann/Corbis

Page 195: Wally McNamee/Corbis

Page 196: AP Images

Pages 200–201: Bettmann/Corbis

Page 202: © Bill Mauldin (1963). Courtesy of the Bill Mauldin Estate LLC

Page 205: LBJ Library photo by Cecil Stoughton

Page 211: Courtesy of Kipp Burgoyne Photography

Page 222 (all): National Archives

Page 223 (all): National Archives

INDEX

Note: Page numbers in **bold** indicate illustrations.

University of Mississippi, 35
U.S. military, expansion of, 23

V

Vice presidents, U.S. *See* Johnson, Lyndon B.; Nixon, Richard M.
Vietnam, U.S. military advisers in, 22–23

W

Walker, Edwin:
    Oswald's attempted assassination of, 56, 58, 59, 75, 77, 97–98, 106
    at political rally, 60
Wallace, George, 35
Warren, Earl, 203, **205**
Warren Commission, 203–207, **205**
Washington, DC, ix, xi, 38, 84. *See also* Capitol, U.S.; Georgetown, Washington, DC; White House
    places to visit in, 225–226
West Germany, 29
White House, 44
    birthday party for John Jr. in, 173, 198
    East Room in, 43, **162**, 163, 164, 173, **174–175**, 177, 182, 188, 226
    funeral preparations in, 172–173, **173**
    JFK lying in state in, 173, **174–175**, 177
    JFK's coffin removed from, 177, **178–179**, 180
    JFK's coffin taken to, 161, **162**, 163, 188
    Johnson's move to, 164–166
    Kennedy family moving out of, 204
    Kennedy residence in, 164–166
    limousine in garage of, 158–159, **159**
    Oval Office in, **44**, 45, 164, 165
    private mass in, 164
    reception of MLK in, 38, **38**
    renovations of, 42, 51
    tours of, 226
    West Wing in, 164–165
World War I, 1, 166
World War II:
    Allies in, 10, 29
    and Arlington National Cemetery, 166
    atomic bombs in, 33
    Axis powers in, 10
    and Berlin, 29, **30**, 31
    and Cold War, 10–11
    Eisenhower in, 8
    end of, 10, 33
    JFK's experiences in, 1, 4–5, **4**, 7, 107
    JFK's survival in, 4–5, 112
    Joe Jr. as pilot in, 1, 5
    Joe Jr.'s death in, 5
    years leading to, 1

Z

Zapruder, Abraham:
    Bell & Howell movie camera of, 101–102, **101**
    and JFK assassination, 105, 106, 109, 110, 112, **116**, **118**, **120**, **218–219**, **220–221**
    and motorcade. *See* and JFK assassination
    movies for sale by, 172
    and timing of shots, **220–221**

ACKNOWLEDGMENTS

This is my third book for young readers. As always, my team of advisers — my wife, Andrea Mays, and our boys, Harrison and Cameron — read and improved the manuscript with numerous suggestions. Andrea read the manuscript several times from first to final draft and enhanced it in countless ways. The boys were nine and eleven when they worked on my first Scholastic book, *Chasing Lincoln's Killer*, and now, at fourteen and sixteen, they are veterans of the publishing process.

I thank my friends Ronald K. L. Collins, Michael F. Bishop, and David Lovett for reading the book prior to its publication and for their helpful comments. David is an expert on the subject, and he owns the largest private library in America on the Kennedy assassination. His expertise was priceless, and on many occasions he shared rare materials from his collection.

My friend and literary agent, Richard Abate, showed remarkable enthusiasm for this book, and gave me the astute advice that young readers want the truth from history, no matter how shocking and sad it might be.

I thank my team at Scholastic, especially my wonderful editor, Dianne Hess, who was with me on this project from the start and who offered many invaluable contributions that made *"The President Has Been Shot!"* a better book. I have fond memories of our countless and illuminating conversations about not only the assassination, but also our mutual fascination with the entire Kennedy era.

I did not believe that Scholastic's Phil Falco, the designer of *Chasing Lincoln's Killer*, could outdo the wonderful cover he created for that book. But he has, and I thank him for his amazing cover and interior design for *"The President Has Been Shot!"* I also thank Alan Gottlieb from the Visual Resources Group at Scholastic for his tenacious work in tracking down the photographs for this book.

The late Wesley J. Liebeler, my professor and mentor at the UCLA School of Law, served as an assistant counsel on the Warren Commission. His insights provided a rare insider's perspective on the investigation of the murder.

Vincent Bugliosi is one of the finest prosecutors in American history; author of one of the most frightening books of the twentieth century, *Helter Skelter: The True Story of the Manson Murders*; and the writer of one of the most important books on the Kennedy assassination. His *Reclaiming History: The Assassination of President John F. Kennedy* is an outspoken and persuasive refutation of the various conspiracy theories that have clouded the history of the event. Vince encouraged me to believe that a young audience would find the story of the death of President Kennedy as compelling as we do.

I can trace the origins of this book back to my childhood. When I was a boy, my mother, Dianne Swanson, led me to what she called her "morgue": a tall, floor-to-ceiling closet with a sliding door that concealed several shelves piled with vintage magazines, illustrated books, newspaper clippings, and photographs. She was a painter, and these were some of her references and sources for ideas. When I was eight or nine years old, I discovered a treasure trove in that closet — her time capsule of materials that she had collected about the assassination of President Kennedy. Mesmerized, I paged through old *Life* and *Look* magazines from the fall of 1963. With care, I opened long-folded newspapers, their pages browned and brittle, that documented the four pivotal days between November 22 and 25 of that year.

My father, Lennart Swanson, shared with me his memories of the day President Kennedy was shot and entranced me with stories about where he was at 12:30 p.m. on November 22, 1963. He also gave me the *Chicago American* newspaper vending rack that I wrote about in this book, and that is, to this day, filled with a stack of copies of the edition from that unforgettable Friday afternoon. So I thank my parents, who inspired me long ago to tell the story that you now hold in your hands.

JAMES L. SWANSON
WASHINGTON, DC | FEBRUARY 12, 2013

ABOUT THE AUTHOR

James L. Swanson is the author of the *New York Times* bestsellers *Manhunt: The 12-Day Chase for Lincoln's Killer* and also its sequel, *Bloody Crimes: The Funeral of Abraham Lincoln and the Chase for Jefferson Davis. Manhunt* won the Edgar Award for the best nonfiction crime book of the year. James's other books include the bestselling classic *Chasing Lincoln's Killer*, an adaptation of *Manhunt* for young readers, and *Bloody Times*, the young adult version of *Bloody Crimes*. His pictorial book *Lincoln's Assassins: Their Trial and Execution* is an acclaimed photo history of the crime, the pursuit of the conspirators, and their fates. James serves on the advisory council of the Ford's Theatre Society. He has degrees in history and law from the University of Chicago and UCLA, and he has held a number of government and think-tank posts in Washington, DC, including at the United States Department of Justice.

Follow him on Twitter @JamesLSwanson.